# In Performance

T0366943

**EDITED BY**
**CAROL MARTIN**

**In Performance** is a book series devoted to national and global theater of the twenty-first century. Scholarly essays providing the theatrical, cultural, and political contexts for the plays and performance texts introduce each volume. The texts are written both by established and emerging writers, translated by accomplished translators and aimed at people who want to put new works on stage, read diverse dramatic and performance literature, and study diverse theater practices, contexts, and histories in light of globalization.

**In Performance** has been supported by translation and editing grants from the following organizations:

The Book Institute, Krakow
TEDA Project, Istanbul
The Memorial Fund for Jewish Culture, New York
Polish Cultural Institute, New York
Zbigniew Raszewski Theatrical Institute, Warsaw
Adam Mickiewicz Institute, Warsaw
Goethe-Institut, New York
Austrian Cultural Forum, New York

# Romina Paula

## FAUNA

### and Other Plays

EDITED BY
**APRIL SWEENEY**
**BRENDA WERTH**

Translated by
BRENDA WERTH
APRIL SWEENEY
JEAN GRAHAM-JONES

Seagull
**BOOKS**

LONDON NEW YORK CALCUTTA

**Seagull Books, 2023**

Plays © Romina Paula

Introduction © Brenda Werth, 2023

Translations © Individual translators

Photographs © Individual photographers and/or theater companies

This compilation © Seagull Books, 2023

ISBN 978 1 8030 9 084 9

**British Library Cataloging-in-Publication Data**
A catalog record for this book is available from the British Library

Book designed by Bishan Samaddar, Seagull Books, Calcutta, India
Printed and bound by Hyam Enterprises, Calcutta, India

# CONTENTS

We are grateful to many people whose crucial support over the years has made possible the publication of *"Fauna" and Other Plays* by Romina Paula. First and foremost, we would like to express our gratitude to Carol Martin, the editor of the In Performance series at Seagull Books, for her dedication to the project and critical insights at every stage of the process. Our heartfelt thanks go out to Bishan Samaddar, who has guided us expertly through the production of the book.

We would like to offer our deepest thanks to Romina Paula, whose beautiful and compelling work inspires and moves so many. She has generously shared her time with us over the last years to discuss the project, in Buenos Aires, New York City, and over many Zoom meetings. We are grateful to the National Endowment of the Arts for awarding us a literary translation fellowship in 2018 to pursue the translation of Paula's play *Fauna*. Without this essential support, the project would not have been possible.

We have also received generous support from our respective universities for this project. Many thanks to the Jack Child Endowment for Latin American Studies at American University and to the Research Council and Division of Arts and Humanities at Colgate University. Our appreciation and admiration go out to Jean Graham-Jones, Paola Hernández, Analola Santana, Cecilia Sosa, Philippa Page, Jordana Blejmar, and Anne García-Romero for being valuable interlocutors and sharing a passion for Romina Paula's work.

We would like to thank Frank Hentschker, executive director and director of programs at the Martin E. Segal Theatre Center at CUNY in New York City, for his enthusiastic early support of the project and for hosting "An Evening with Romina Paula" at the Segal Center in

December 2019. We are deeply grateful for his commitment to promoting Paula's work.

We are indebted to the numerous artists in New York City who have contributed their time, energy, and talent in supporting our efforts to bring this work into English through readings and rehearsals during our translation process—including the generosity and tenacity of Jose Scaro, Ben Becher, and Tony Torn for their help in bringing these works to audiences in 2022.

Lastly, thanks to our colleagues in Buenos Aires: Luciana Acuña, Luis Biasotto, Federico Léon, Shoshana Polanco, Paula Santamaría, Matías Sendón, Bruno Savransky, Carolina Sotolano, Jorge Dubatti, Lorena Verzero, Emilio Crenzel, Grisby Ogás Puga, Carolina Soler, and many others who have shared their kindness, spirit, and extra-ordinary work over the years, continually connecting us, literally and figuratively, to a rich and diverse landscape of culture and artistic production. And on a personal note, we respectively thank Matthew Miller and Mark Wright, each for their unyielding support and engagement in all of our endeavors.

*April Sweeney and Brenda Werth*

## REWILDING THE POETICS OF LOVE, LIFE, AND INTIMACY IN ROMINA PAULA'S THEATER

Brenda Werth

Romina Paula is one of Argentina's most celebrated playwrights, winning critical acclaim both at home and abroad. Her carefully crafted and textually sophisticated plays move us to think about how we tell the stories of people's lives. They offer nuanced explorations of gender, sexuality, feminism, and family. This volume presents the first English-language translation of *The Sound It Makes* (2007), *The Whole of Time* (2009), *Fauna* (2013), and *Rewilding* (2016). The plays defy traditional boundaries between the arts by engaging the different modes of production and the languages of theater, film, dance, music, and the visual arts. Her work explores the synergies between documentary and fiction, gender and biography, and the relationship between life, love, and art.[1] Paula is a playwright and also a theater director, film actor, filmmaker, and novelist, and her work across genres has inspired new dramaturgy and fostered a dynamic community of theater and film practitioners in Argentina.

---

**1** Not included here is Paula's first play, *Si te sigo, muero* (If I follow you, I die, 2005), a collaborative creation with the Grupo Febrero that draws heavily on the poetic texts of the writer Viel Temperley. Paula's recent play, *Reinos* (Kingdoms), which premiered at the Sarmiento Theater in Buenos Aires in 2019, is also the result of collective collaboration with artists Agustina Muñoz and Margarita Molfino. Based on the diary of Molfino's grandmother, written between 1934 and 1942, the play provides an intimate exploration of gender, work, and nature, but turns specifically to the question of inheritance and how certain experiences, expectations, and forms of knowledge are acquired and discarded over time and across generations.

Paula's work is in dialogue with current theater trends in Argentina's shifting political, economic, and cultural landscape over the last several decades. In the broadest of terms, her work belongs to Argentina's post-dictatorship period, which spans from 1983 to the present and includes the transition to democracy, the deepening of neoliberalism in the 1990s, the crushing economic collapse of 2001, the reopening of human rights trials, a decade of social democracy under the former presidents and husband-and-wife team, Néstor Kirchner and Cristina Fernández de Kirchner (2003–2015), followed by a return to neoliberalism under President Mauricio Macri (2015–2019). The presidential election of 2019 signaled yet another return of the Kirchnerist brand of Peronism under President Alberto Fernández. In the twenty-first century, laws supporting marriage equality, gender identity rights, and protection against gender violence and human trafficking have made Argentina a leader in the advocacy of gender and sexuality justice fueled by spectacular protests against gender violence and in defense of reproductive rights led by the movements NiUnaMenos and the Green Tide, respectively.

Argentine theater makers who were born during the transition to democracy are frequently interested in exploring memory, both inherited and experiential. Their work shows continuity with the groundbreaking theater movement Teatro Abierto (1981–1985) and its powerful denunciation of the military dictatorship (1976–1983), but their treatment of memory and violence is more subtle and varied. From the late 1980s to mid-90s Teatro Abierto, along with groups such as El periférico de objetos, and plays such as *Furious Antigone* (1986) by Griselda Gambaro, exposed and denounced the oppression, violence, and corruption of the dictatorship. They provided testimony to account for the dead and disappeared, but, according to Jean Graham-Jones in her discussion of Teatro Abierto, plays were not always able to escape the binary logic of the representation of perpetrators and victims.[2] In contrast, the theater of the late 90s and the early twenty-first century is focused on exploring nuanced, playful, and less reverent depictions of the past. This theater is still very much affectively linked to the events of dictatorship but driven less by a desire to uphold heroic portrayals of militancy.[3]

Paula's generation of theater makers questions normative models of family, representing a significant break with both traditional representations of family in the canon of Argentine theater and with the conservative image of family imposed by the military junta during the dictatorship.[4] Emblematic works of the Río de la Plata region such as Florencio Sánchez's *La gringa* (1904), Armando Discépolo's *grotesco criollo* masterpiece *Stéfano* (1928), and Roberto Cossa's realist work *Nuestro fin de semana* (Our Weekend, 1964) played a critical role in consolidating national identity through the representation of the Argentine family. No matter how uniquely dysfunctional the families portrayed, they upheld an image of the traditional nuclear family as the basic unit of the nation. The traditional nuclear family was also crucial to the military junta's campaign to promote a Western, Christian, and conservative image of the family/nation, controlled by a strong paternal figure and nurtured by a submissive maternal figure.[5] The Mothers of Plaza de Mayo created a difficult situation for the military when they began publicly marching in the late 70s demanding

*xi*

INTRODUCTION

**2** Jean Graham-Jones, *Exorcising History: Argentine Theater under Dictatorship* (Lewisburg, PA: Bucknell University Press, 2000), p. 121.

**3** Jordana Blejmar, *Playful Memories: The Autofictional Turn in Post-dictatorship Argentina* (Cham: Springer International Publishing, 2018).

**4** Cecilia Sosa, *Queering Acts Mourning in the Aftermath of Argentina's Dictatorship: The Performances of Blood* (Suffolk: Tamesis, 2014).

**5** Diana Taylor, *Disappearing Acts: Spectacles of Gender and Nationalism in Argentina's "Dirty War"* (Durham, NC: Duke University Press, 1997).

to know what happened to their disappeared children. Though activists were individually targeted, the military could not repress the Mothers' collective demonstrations because the regime had already enshrined mothers as virtuous and fundamental to the well-being of the nation. The Mothers' activism marks a pivotal moment when women began to engage politically in the public sphere in Argentina. The collective force they embodied would be revived again in the mass mobilization of the NiUnaMenos marches against gender violence that began in 2015. In addition to the Mothers, the Grandmothers of Plaza de Mayo and the Children for Identity and Justice, Against Forgetting and Silence (H.I.J.O.S.), are major human rights organizations that emerged in the wake of dictatorship.[6] Like the Mothers, these organizations are structured around demands linked to family identity. The Grandmothers, in particular, have worked tirelessly to recover the identities of the over 500 babies that were stolen during dictatorship, and have had to rely on bloodlines, quite literally, through genetic analysis in order to identify these stolen individuals. Attentive to the role of familism in coming to terms with the past, a new generation of theater makers proposes alternative family models and ways of belonging in their work.[7]

Argentina's recent history shows the intersection of the country's neoliberal agenda and the continuing violent effects of dictatorship long after regime change and transition to democracy. During the last military dictatorship, the economics minister José Alfredo Martínez de Hoz set the country on a neoliberal track that was further consolidated under democracy during the presidency of Carlos Saúl

---

**6** Grandchildren of the generation of the disappeared formed the organization Nietes (Grandchildren) in 2020, during the COVID-19 pandemic.

**7** Sosa, *Queering Acts Mourning*; Kerry Bystrom, "The Public Private Sphere: Family Narrative and Democracy in Argentina and South Africa," *Social Dynamics* 36(1) (2010): 139–52.

Menem (1989–1999). Menem's embrace of neoliberal policies directly led to the country's devastating economic collapse of 2001, resulting in political turmoil, a radical devaluation of the peso, the confiscation of Argentines' savings, and a dramatic increase in the percentage of Argentines living in poverty. The crisis produced an environment of profound political, social, and bodily precarity. Argentines gathered in the streets banging pots and pans together in their trademark *cacerolazos*, demanding that the politicians all leave: "que se vayan todos." Meanwhile, families and individuals referred to as *cartoneros*, forced into extreme poverty, combed the streets in the middle of the night looking for cardboard (*cartón*) and other recyclable items to sell. Theater scholar Jorge Dubatti identifies a preoccupation with biopolitics as one of the predominant themes in Argentine theater produced in the early twenty-first century, a direct result of the sense of bodily precarity generated by the economic crisis.[8] And in her analysis of theater in Buenos Aires after 2001, Graham-Jones considers movements such as Theater for Identity (Teatroxlaidentidad) and the rapid development of community-based theater (*teatro comunitario*) examples of "horizontalist, self-generative approaches to cultural practices that accompanied the political, economic, and social restructuring attempted in response to the national crisis."[9] During this time, artists became adept at devising improvisational strategies in both creating and producing their work; and they often worked in multiple arenas and across genres in order to make ends meet.

8 Jorge Dubatti, "El teatro de Buenos Aires en el siglo XXI: pluralismo, canon 'imposible' y post-neoliberalismo," *Latin American Theatre Review* 45(1) (2011): 45–73; here, p. 46.
9 Jean Graham-Jones, "Rethinking Buenos Aires Theatre in the Wake of 2001 and Emerging Structures of Resistance and Resilience." *Theatre Journal* 66(1) (2014): 37–54; here, p. 39. See also Marina Sitrin's concepts of *horizontalidad* and *autogestión* in *Horizontalism: Voices of Popular Power in Argentina* (Oakland, CA: AK Press, 2006).

In the wake of the economic crisis, a generation of artists began to borrow and combine techniques from theater, film, photography, dance, and music.[10] "When we started studying acting, film and theater were two separate spheres . . . ," Paula notes. "That has changed completely, and now there is a natural circulation between the two spaces."[11] In 2011, Paula starred in Santiago Mitre's film *The Student,* and began working closely with Argentine filmmaker Matías Piñeiro, acting in all three of his Shakespeare-inspired trilogy of films: *Rosalinda* (2010), *Viola* (2012), and *The Princess of France* (2014). She wrote and directed her first film, *De nuevo otra vez* (*Again Once Again*) in 2019, in which she also stars along with her mother and son. Despite her increasing presence in film, Paula nonetheless feels that she belongs in independent theater where artists are "united by a shared mode of production." For Paula, independent theater in Buenos Aires works almost like a cooperative: there is little or no money, but everyone gets a share. According to Paula, multitasking is good for artists, because of the dialogue and contagion that result from cross-disciplinary work.[12] She embodies what Jordana Blejmar and Cecilia Sosa call "a fresh and exciting generational, transnational, and trans-disciplinary voice within Argentine performing arts."[13]

---

10 In their recent work, Jordana Blejmar, Philippa Page, and Cecilia Sosa examine the hybridity between screen and stage in twenty-first century Argentine performance, focusing on Romina Paula, Lola Arias, Mariano Pensotti, Alejo Moguillansky, Matías Piñeiro, among others. In Blejmar, Page, and Sosa, *Entre/telones y pantallas: afectos y saberes en la performance argentina contemporánea* (Buenos Aires: Libraria, 2020).

11 Mercedes Halfon, "Cerca del corazón salvaje," interview with Romina Paula, *Página 12* (May 26, 2013). Available at: https://bit.ly/3EuLQSj (this and subsequent weblinks last accessed on October 11, 2022).

12 Romina Paula, "Writing in Buenos Aires" (Jennifer Croft trans.), *Berfrois* (May 22, 2018). Available at: https://bit.ly/3CoGW6P

13 Jordana Blejmar and Cecilia Sosa, "Theater on Screen, Cinema on Stage: Cross-Genre Imaginaries in Contemporary Argentina Introduction," *Latin American Theatre Review* 50(2) (2017): 9-21; here p. 9.

Though in many ways Paula's work is representative of this new generation of interdisciplinary and genre-defying artists, her theater marks a notable departure from the significant body of work that emerged in the 90s exploring documentary modes and the real, first in Vivi Tellas's work and a decade later in the work of Lola Arias, Federico León, Mariano Pensotti, and Grupo Krapp, among others.[14] Describing Paula's dramaturgy, Dubatti writes, "those who speak of the death of representation or of the postdramatic will soon realize that those categories are not valid for the theater of Romina Paula, which multiplies the power of fiction, the thickness of great dramatic situations, and recovers storytelling, emotion, and the monumentality of character."[15] While Paula engages trends currently popular in Argentina, such as Tellas's biodramas and other modes of documentary theater, she is ultimately more interested in reflecting on the blurriness between fiction and the real in conversation with audiences about what constitutes art, acting, experience, and identity.

## THE PLAYWRIGHT

Paula's plays are broadly influenced by Argentine literature, contemporary North American theater, the visual arts, pop culture, and German romanticism. In *Rewilding*, she uses the idea of hyperlinks to weave intertexts into a coherent universe. Her plays are frequently in dialogue with one or more famous works, such as Tennessee Williams's *The Glass Menagerie* in *The Whole of Time*, and Jorge Luis Borges's short story "The Intruder" in *The Sound It Makes*.

---

**14** See Carol Martin, *Theatre of the Real* (Basingstoke: Palgrave Macmillan, 2015); *Dramaturgy of the Real on the World Stage* (Basingstoke: Palgrave Macmillan, 2012); Paola S. Hernández, *Staging Lives in Latin American Theater: Bodies, Objects, Archives* (Evanston, IL: Northwestern University Press, 2021).
**15** Jorge Dubatti, "El teatro de Buenos Aires en el siglo XXI," p. 63 (my translation).

Both a tribute to and a critique of these canonical works, Paula radically adapts them by identifying and questioning the patriarchal structures contained in them. In other cases, she references works that hold resonance in the present moment, such as Frida Kahlo's painting *A Few Small Nips*, or Sarah Ruhl's *Late: A Cowboy Song*, works that touch on themes related to gender violence and explore shifts in gender identity and definitions of family. A tribute to her love of literature and the visual arts, Paula's intertextuality also reflects her obsession with time: "I think about how to narrate simultaneity: it's impossible. According to our perception of time and space, one thing happens after another. Language is successive, history is successive, but what about time?"[16] Paula uses intertextuality to disrupt linear moments in time.[17] Through citation, she brings other authors, words, and ideas into her own work, creating a kind of coexistence in a productive limbo.[18]

Paula's trajectories as playwright and novelist have developed in parallel and in dialogue with one another. Any discussion of the influences on Paula's work must take into account the impact her work as a novelist has had on her theater. Paula has published three novels: *¿Vos me querés a mí?* (And you, do you love me? 2005); *Agosto* (August, 2009) and *Acá todavía* (Still Here, 2016), as well as several essays, and a collection of short stories, *Archivos de Word* (Word Archives, 2021). *Agosto* was translated into English as *August* by Jennifer Croft and published by the Feminist Press at CUNY in 2017. Paula's writing process gives us clues as to why she was ultimately drawn to theater.

---

**16** Roger Koza, "La crisis de los 40, según Romina Paula," interview with Romina Paula, *Revista Ñ. Clarín* (June 7, 2019). Available at: https://bit.ly/3TaOFMp

**17** Darren Hughes, "'I Love Silence, and I Like to Be Bored': Romina Paula on Her Rotterdam-Premiering Directorial Debut, *Again Once Again*," interview with Romina Paula, *Filmmaker* (February 18, 2019). Available at: https://bit.ly/3CoJuls

**18** Halfon, "Cerca del corazón salvaje."

In an interview for the literary journal *Berfrois*, she says she attended writing workshops where she was an "avid, almost frenzied writer," eager to learn new literary techniques, but that she eventually started to write dialogue almost exclusively, incorporating excerpts from her diaries.[19] This dialogic structure and the use of the second person are prominent in *¿Vos me querés a mí?* and *Agosto*. Argentine play-wright Mauricio Kartún once commented that Paula writes theater as if it were narrative and novels as if they were theater.[20] Indeed, while her novels are praised for their unique use of dialogue, her plays are often complexly interwoven with literary intertexts.

Even when Paula's intertexts verge on becoming unwieldy, her fast-moving dialogue is clever and ironic, and occasionally absurd, but unfailingly witty. In the first scene of *Fauna*, for example, a dialogue between three main characters discussing the creation of a film about Fauna's life shows how Paula uses citation and metatheatrical techniques in humorous dialogue.

> **ACTRESS.** "But as you left, the stage cracked . . ."
>
> **DIRECTOR.** Yeah, right there.
>
> **MARÍA LUISA.** But that's a metaphor. It's talking about death, "Death Experience." The stage referred to is the stage of life. It's a familiar trope, you know, that all the world's a stage. It's in Shakespeare and Calderón, it's an Elizabethan trope.
>
> **DIRECTOR.** Okay, okay, thanks. I'm not saying it isn't, but what I'm saying is that I don't think it works for us, as interesting as it may be, but thanks anyway. I think it's better to stick to her story.

**19** Paula, "Writing in Buenos Aires."

**20** Ivanna Soto, "Cuestiones con el amor y con la vida," *Clarín: Revista Ñ* (October 25, 2016). Available at: https://bit.ly/3CkyB3S

**MARÍA LUISA.** Fauna loved Rilke.

**DIRECTOR.** Yes, but, um . . . how should I put this, the truth doesn't necessarily matter, María Luisa.

Paula wrote and directed all four plays included in this volume. *The Sound It Makes* (2007), *The Whole of Time* (2009), and *Fauna* (2013) she wrote and directed in collaboration with the theater company El Silencio, founded together with Pilar Gamboa and Esteban Bigliardi in 2006. Two actors later joined the company: Susana Pampín arrived for their second production, and Rafael Ferro came on board during rehearsals for *Fauna*. All three plays produced by El Silencio were staged at El Callejón de Deseos in Buenos Aires, an intimate and versatile performance space in the Abasto neighborhood, known for its experimental, underground theater venues. Though Paula shares that she and the actors spent a good amount of time laughing together during rehearsals, the experience of staging *Fauna* ended the collaborative work of El Silencio.[21] After the run of *Fauna* concluded, the theater closed, and Paula was pregnant, a combination of factors that she says created a sense of closure for the group.[22]

The plays included in this volume trace this trajectory of Paula's work from realist to more abstract work. Paula considers the trilogy of plays she created with El Silencio to be fundamentally realist. Even *Fauna*, with its minimalist stage design, features characters with first and last names, biographies, and psychological development.[23] After *Fauna*, Paula's work became less structured and more abstract. *Rewilding* (2016), the fourth play in this volume, marks a departure in

**21** Alejandro Cruz, "Una fauna y sus faunos," *La Nación* (May 21, 2013). Available at: https://bit.ly/3SOO8NY

**22** *Revista Cabal*, "Entrevista a la dramaturga Romina Paula." Available at: https://bit.ly/3CsaD79

**23** Paula Sabatés, "Teatro con estructura de hipervínculos," *Página 12* (July 13, 2017). Available at: https://bit.ly/3CRLvbc

Paula's work and a shift toward a more conceptual vision of theater. In an interview, Paula confesses that she doesn't know what the play is or what it might become.[24] There is no classical narrative structure and character development is minimal. To one side of the stage is a pyramid of wooden crates; to the other is a painting by an unknown artist. Premiered at the Argentine Theater Center for Experimentation and Creation in La Plata, Argentina, the theater's brutalist architecture and expansive stage space gave the performance an uncontained, limitless feel. Actors explore with experimental movement as they discuss love, art, poetry, gender, family, and philosophy. *Rewilding* culminates a process of abstraction in Paula's work and reveals her interest in cultivating a more personal experience for audience members that is less structured, more open-ended, and perhaps even wilder.

Paula belongs to a generation of writers influenced by feminist thought and a tide of activism sometimes referred to in Argentina as "the revolution of the daughters." This generation expresses new perspectives on gender, sexuality, and reproductive rights, which resonate with transnational movements such as #NiUnaMenos and #MeToo, and the emergence of the fourth wave of feminism, especially its focus on oppressive gender norms, intersectionality, a critique of interlocking systems of power, and social media as a powerful tool of activism. Influences in Paula's work include Concepción Arenal, María Luisa Bemberg, Dorothea Lange, Katherine Anne Porter, Flora Tristan, Sarah Ruhl, and others. In *Fauna*, for example, Paula names the character of Fauna's daughter María Luisa, evoking the Argentine feminist filmmaker María Luisa Bemberg. Though Paula employs intertextual techniques, she also historicizes the multiple strands of feminist thought originating in distinct contexts. When asked if the themes she chooses to highlight in her work could be considered a

---

**24** Sabatés, "Teatro con estructura de hipervínculos."

form of activism, Paula responds that she does not. She selects specific themes out of a personal need to write about them.[25] More than an activist impulse, what drives Paula's work is the desire to explore themes of femininity and masculinity and the fluidity of gender and sexual identity. Her reflections on gender identity are most developed in the last two plays in this volume, *Fauna* and *Rewilding*, whereas *The Sound It Makes* and *The Whole of Time* explore gender violence by establishing dialogue with works that either offer narratives of violence against women (Borges's "The Intruder") or document it visually (Frida Kahlo's *A Few Small Nips*). A frequent strategy in Paula's work, evident in the first three plays of this volume, is the development of an inquisitive character who questions and disrupts existing patriarchal structures, patterns of violence, and gender expectations. In *The Sound It Makes*, Mariana doubles as a detective, determined to uncover the repressed secret of the two brothers. In *The Whole of Time*, Antonia proves to be an unsettling presence through her rejection of prescribed gender roles and her insistence on living on her own terms. In *Fauna*, Julia reflects on how the fluidity of gender affects how lives are narrated and questions the choice to be a mother.

Present throughout Paula's dramatic works is her fascination with the double, and the cultivation and frustration of identification between two characters. In *Fauna*, for example, Fauna becomes Fauno and Julia begins dressing like a man to satisfy her intense desire to know Fauna. Likewise in *Rewilding*, Paula juxtaposes the figures of Chabuca Granda and Lucha Reyes, Peruvian songwriter and singer respectively, who come together despite differences in class and race, to write and perform the songs "Cinnamon Flower" and "José Antonio," respectively. At other times this doubling is more sinister.

---

25 Liliana Viola, "Se cae de madura," *Página 12* (December 4, 2009). Available at: https://bit.ly/3EBLeuq

In *The Sound It Makes*, an uncanny doubling occurs between the two brothers, who share an eerie resemblance. Paula's play alludes to the possibility that like in Borges's short story "The Intruder," the two brothers are complicit in a violent crime. In *Rewilding*, Gabi's description of her brother's return from the woods evokes a frightening double: "It's not that he was different or changed. He was something else entirely. An Other that invaded our family and devoured it from the inside out."

Paula's interest in the wild and savage resonates with nineteenth-century discourse on civilization and barbarism in Latin America. A nod to this discourse can be seen in *Fauna* in the explicit reference to the character Horacio Quiroga, the Uruguayan author who wrote short stories about the littoral region of Argentina, where *Fauna* is set. Not coincidentally, Fauna's last name is Forteza, also the second last name of the writer (Horacio Silvestre Quiroga Forteza). Influenced by Edgar Allen Poe, Jack London, and Rudyard Kipling, Quiroga's modernist works contain elements of the fantastic, tragic, and supernatural in stories such as "La gallina degollada" (The Decapitated Chicken). The scene in *Fauna* in which two mares are devoured by a swarm of bees gestures to Quiroguian themes and aesthetics.

While Paula's theater is in dialogue with Latin American writers and literary discourse, it is also influenced by German literature. One of Paula's greatest interlocutors, especially in *Fauna* and *Rewilding*, is Rainer Maria Rilke, whose reflections on art, identity, love, and death are central to her work. In *Rewilding*, references to Caspar David Friedrich and Heinrich von Kleist signal the influence of the German Romanticists as does Paula's fascination with the uncanny, a frequent sensation produced by Paula's plays.[26] Paula's cultivation of intimate

---

26 Laurie R. Johnson, Aesthetic Anxiety: Uncanny Symptoms in German Literature and Culture (Amsterdam: Rodopi, 2010).

family settings while simultaneously disrupting them de-familiarizes the family. Her questioning of traditional conceptions of family, gender, and sexuality deepens over the course of her plays and corresponds to a shift in scenic design from more naturalist, familial settings, found in *The Sound It Makes* and *The Whole of Time*, to the minimalist and abstract environments in *Fauna* and *Rewilding*.

## THE PLAYS

*The Sound It Makes* tells the story of two reclusive brothers living in a resort town off Argentina's Atlantic coast. Premiering at the Callejón de Deseos Theater, Buenos Aires, in 2007, the play was also performed at the Fourth International Theater Festival in Buenos Aires (FIBA), and toured internationally in Spain and Brazil. As in Borges's short story "The Intruder," on which the play is loosely based, the two brothers exhibit a pathological closeness. In the Borges original, the brothers fall in love with the same woman, a housekeeper they have invited into their home, and whom they later murder because she has threatened their relationship. Like in Borges's short story, in *The Sound It Makes* the intruder is a woman, in this case an inquisitive cousin. She arrives at the brothers' home, asks probing questions about their past in an attempt to reveal the brothers' involvement in their mother's death and a violent act carried out against a girlfriend. Paula's play introduces a feminist reading of Borges's haunting tale, in which a socially and economically vulnerable woman is murdered in order to preserve the brothers' relationship. In Paula's play the woman has the upper hand as her scrutiny unsettles the brothers' world and holds them accountable. The play's repressed acts of violence, pact of silence, and sinister ambience are all emblematic themes in post-dictatorship cultural production. Mariana's constant questioning alludes to the importance of truth seeking and coming to terms with past violence.

*The Whole of Time* builds on and expands the intertextual richness of *The Sound It Makes* to include visual and musical texts, most prominently by Mexican artists, including Frida Kahlo, the singer-songwriter Marco Antonio Solís, and singer Chavela Vargas. Inspired by Tennessee Williams's *The Glass Menagerie*, the play references the popular myth that the Mexican singer Solís murdered his wife. Other references include Kahlo's painting *A Few Small Nips* (1935), a visual documentation of a femicide that took place in Mexico; and a highly publicized case of familicide that took place in 1992 in Argentina. In the play, the twenty-something Antonia implores her mother to stop asking her to find a boyfriend. While the overall plot, family structure and characters are inspired by *The Glass Menagerie*, Paula complicates Antonia's fragility by giving her a strong and lucid voice, which she uses to argue why she would prefer not to have a boyfriend. Placing Antonia in dialogue with Frida Kahlo and Chavela Vargas, women who defied societal expectations, Paula creates a feminist hero with an alternative family. Premiering at the Callejón de Deseos Theater in Buenos Aires in 2010, *The Whole of Time* won the Florencio Sánchez Prize for best Argentine play, and in 2011 it took part in the prestigious Theater du Rond Festival in Paris. In 2012, the play continued to tour as part of the Santiago a Mil festival in Chile and the Napoli Teatro Festival in Italy, and in 2013 it premiered in Girona, Spain and throughout France in Aix-en-Provence, Arles, Pau, Toulouse, Montbéliard, Corsica, and Montpellier.

*Fauna* is about the making of a film that will never be completed, a film that brings together a daughter, a son, an actress, and a director to tell the story of Fauna, legendary figure who in her lifetime dressed like a man, translated Rilke, and rode her horse with abandon until she was in her nineties. The play premiered at the General San Martín Cultural Center in Buenos Aires in 2013 and has toured internationally throughout Latin America and Europe, taking part in the Festival d'Automne in Paris in 2013. Highly intertextual, reflexive, and subtly ironic, the play explores how to tell the story of one's life, how to capture what is true and real, and how to decipher where reality ends and fiction begins. Central to this exploration is the theme of how gender fluidity impacts the ways in which life narratives are imagined and rendered artistically. As the characters discuss how best to represent the life of Fauna, a shifting, multivalent romantic tension emerges. The tension manifests itself when characters take turns rehearsing scenes from Fauna's life, casting off prescriptive notions of gender roles as they do so. The play ends with all of the characters caught in an intricate web of emotion and desire, leaving audiences with a complex, multiple, and unpredictable vision of love. In contrast to the intensity of emotion displayed by the characters, the stage itself is austere and minimalist in design. Envisioned for a black box theater, the floor of the square-shaped stage space is covered by weathered wooden planks. At stage left toward the back, there is a wooden table fastened with a saddle. The scenic design reflects a departure in Paula's work—an attempt to move away from naturalist tropes and more normative representations of family found in *The Sound It Makes* and *The Whole of Time*. This spatial and familial abstraction reaches its culmination in the last play of the volume, *Rewilding*.

*Rewilding* premiered at the Teatro Argentino in La Plata in 2016 and had subsequent runs in Buenos Aires at the Cervantes Theater in 2017 and the Zelaya Theater in 2018. *Rewilding* picks up where *Fauna* leaves off, abstracting the dialogue between characters to the point that the play becomes largely conceptual, driven not by narrative but by hyperlinks that, according to Paula, connect characters' reflections, guiding audiences on an intuitive and experimental journey. Her exploration of what is considered wild and untamed reveals a desire to question convention, in relation not only to gender norms but also to theater. The focus on hyperlinks departs from classic narrative structure and disrupts traditional conceptions of time and definitions of realism resulting in a radical questioning of conventions of theater, language, gender, family, and love. In *Rewilding,* Paula weaves on a diverse set of influences including Sarah Ruhl's *Late: A Cowboy Song,* the eighteenth-century German Sturm und Drang movement, and Rainer Maria Rilke's poem "Letters to a Young Poet."

Paula's plays imagine worlds that are both poetically expansive and intimate. Her complex stories create unexpected and emotionally intense connections between characters and audiences. She moves audiences to think about how we tell the stories of people's lives, and the role of art in constructing and deconstructing ideas about love, family, and gender. Her plays stretch and collapse the time between past and present through the sophisticated interweaving of literary texts, myths, fairy tales, and the visual arts. Paula invites audiences to reflect on how the current global moment must address structural violence and gender inequity by recognizing how shifting conceptions of family, gender, and sexuality have revolutionized the public sphere in Argentina, US, and around the world.

THE SOUND IT MAKES

*The Sound It Makes* won the 2006 Metrovías Prize and premiered at Espacio Callejón in Buenos Aires as part of the 2007 VI Festival Internacional de Buenos Aires. The play was directed by Romina Paula with set design by Juliana Iriart and Matías Sendón, lighting design by Matías Sendón, costume design by Glenda Lloyd, sound design by Ignacio Bouquet, and choreography by Manuel Attwell.

## CAST

| | |
|---:|:---|
| **COLO** | Esteban Bigliardi |
| **NACHO** | Esteban Lamothe |
| **MARIANA** | Pilar Gamboa |

TRANSLATED BY **April Sweeney** AND **Brenda Werth**

*This, and other things we do not know, helps to explain how close
they were; to cross one of them meant having two enemies.*[1]

Jorge Luis Borges, "The Intruder"

## I. MUSIC

*Miramar. The living room of a stately home. Two well-dressed brothers
with an air of wealth, in symbiotic existence. It's autumn, and in autumn
it's cold near the sea. Colo writes in his notebook. Nacho listens to music.*

**COLO.** Can you turn it down a little?

**NACHO.** Fine, but there's no way that could possibly bother you. Any
softer and you wouldn't hear a thing.

**COLO.** I can't concentrate like this. It's right in my ear.

**NACHO.** Well, then move over a little.

**COLO.** I don't want to move over. I was here first. Besides, I'm doing
something useful.

**NACHO.** What does that have to do with anything? Do whatever you
want. I won't bother you. I'm just playing a little music.

**COLO.** Yes, but you know that I can't concentrate like this.

**NACHO.** Just because you're doing something doesn't mean that I can't
be doing something else at the same time. That's not fair.

**COLO.** Nacho, you can do whatever you want as long as it doesn't make
noise. Read, if you want, or go outside.

---

**1** Jorge Luis Borges, "The Intruder" (1966) (Alastair Reid trans.), *Encounter* (April 1969):
15–17; here, p. 15.

NACHO. I don't want to go outside. I want to listen to music. You're the one who should have to leave. If you're so intent on writing, go upstairs. This area is for living.

*Colo puts up with the music for a few more seconds, then stops and turns down the volume. Nacho also stands up. They go back and forth turning the volume up and down. Nacho grabs his brother violently and turns off the radio. Colo goes back to his notebook.*

COLO. Nacho, at the house in Rumipal, were the beds beside each other or one on top of the other?

NACHO. What?

COLO. Our beds, were they bunked or side by side?

NACHO. I don't know. I think at first they were bunk beds and then they sawed them in half because the space between the beds was too small. I think. (*Colo is no longer listening; he returns to writing in his notebook.*) Are you going to put that sweater on, or are you just holding it to hold it?

COLO. Why?

NACHO. I'm going into town. Can I have it?

COLO. When you leave I'll give it to you.

NACHO. I'm going now. I'm leaving. (*Colo doesn't resist too much. He's concentrating. He takes off his sweater. Nacho takes off what he has on and he gives it to Colo. They put on each other's clothes. Sweater choreography. In front of the mirror.*) Is this the inside or outside?

COLO. Inside. (*He helps his brother put it on.*)

## II. MARIANA

*The brothers and their cousin walk in. Choreography. They stop and turn. They look at her. They're uncomfortable.*

MARIANA. You're exactly the same.

(*They look at their clothes.*)

Like a little bigger, but the same.

(*She takes a little stroll around the room and looks up the stairway.*)

You haven't changed a thing.

(*Silence*)

I wanted to apologize for not being able to come before now. The truth is that I just couldn't.

(*They look at her.*)

It wasn't easy for me, okay, for anyone, least of all for you two, I imagine, but you were already here. I was going through a difficult time in my life, and, the truth is, I couldn't bring myself to come.

(*Silence.*) I also wasn't getting along with my mother very well, and when she told me she was coming, I didn't want to come with her. I thought about the car trip with her and, honestly, I just couldn't. I was going through a breakup and my mind was elsewhere. It hit me hard. The truth is in the end I also felt like dying. (*They look at her.*)

How are you guys?

NACHO. Good.

COLO. Good, yeah.

MARIANA. Good. Of course, the great thing is that you have each other, that's what's great. It was terrible for me. I was very alone, but *alone* alone, you know.

NACHO. Why didn't you come?

MARIANA. I don't know, I couldn't. I just explained to you that I wasn't well.

(*Silence.*)

You guys are beautiful, hmm. Colo, you're good-looking. You've grown a lot.

**NACHO.** That's Colo.

**MARIANA.** Really? You're identical. It's like you're carbon copies. No, you, you're redder.

**NACHO.** A little.

**COLO.** A little, yeah.

*Silence.*

**NACHO.** Are you on vacation?

**MARIANA.** No, I don't know, I'm going to stay a few days. I wanted to see you. I can stay here, right? I tried to let you know but I couldn't get through. Don't you pick up?

**NACHO.** It doesn't ring.

**COLO.** You could have let us know.

**MARIANA.** I tried to call you but I couldn't get through.

*Colo goes to check his notebook and returns.*

**COLO.** When Mariana was a kid she wore the ugliest clothes.

**MARIANA.** What?

**COLO.** The clothes you used to wear were hideous.

**MARIANA.** Okay, but I didn't dress myself. They dressed me. They dressed all of us. I didn't choose. And neither did you, they dressed you too.

**COLO.** No, I refused. I didn't let them put just anything on me. I decided. I had an opinion.

**MARIANA.** Fine, whatever. It just seems to me that the two of you didn't dress yourselves very well either. That's all I'm saying.

**COLO.** You were the youngest, right?

NACHO. Yes. Aunt Maruca's daughter.

(*Colo looks at him.*)

The redhead. The aunt with the red hair.

COLO. Ah, right.

MARIANA. You all used to dress badly, it was pretty ugly. Look at the way you put on that sweater, Ignacio.

NACHO. My what?

MARIANA. Your sweater.

NACHO. This? This is Ralph Lauren.

MARIANA. Okay, but don't wear it tucked in.

*Silence.*

NACHO. Are you going to stay for long?

MARIANA. I don't know. A few days, whatever it takes. I can stay here, right?

*The boys look at each other.*

NACHO. Here? No . . . There's no room.

MARIANA. I can't stay upstairs?

NACHO. Upstairs? No, I'd have to move a ton of stuff.

COLO. Are you here on vacation?

MARIANA. Well, sort of. No. Actually, I want to look into renting something.

COLO. Something like what?

NACHO. I can take you. I can show you some places. We've got everything here: apartments, bungalows, duplexes—new, old, whatever. I guess it depends on what you're looking for. There are some that are cheap, they're inland, and there are some with an ocean view but they're more expensive.

MARIANA. I don't know. I have seven hundred pesos.[2] I want to put down a deposit and then I'll see. I want to leave Buenos Aires.

COLO. Seven hundred?

MARIANA. Uh-huh.

COLO. You have it here?

MARIANA. Yes.

COLO. Will you show us?

MARIANA. What do you want to see it for?

COLO. I want to see it. I want to see all of it at once.

MARIANA. Why? What do you want to see it for? I told you I have it.

COLO. I just want to see it. I want to see it all at once. It's been a long time since I've seen seven hundred pesos all together.

MARIANA. Okay.

(*She makes a show of it, like she's going to take out the money. She takes out her wallet but at the very last second changes her mind.*)

Why would I show you the seven hundred pesos? If I told you that I have the money, I have it, period. I don't understand why you want to see it.

COLO. Why does it matter? I just want to see it.

*Colo tries to check her bag and she pushes him away. Nacho reacts by grabbing her arm violently.*

NACHO. You have to calm down.

*A moment of tension. Colo hesitates for a few moments, grabs his notebook and begins to write. She laughs to diffuse the situation.*

MARIANA. The thing is, he touched my stuff . . .

NACHO. You have to calm down. Let's go for a walk.

---

2 At the time of the premiere, 700 Argentine pesos would have been worth around 250 US dollars, so it is meant to be a substantial amount of money.

MARIANA. Later. I'm dead tired. I want to rest for a while. Would you mind taking my things upstairs?

NACHO. Sure, I'll take them up right now.

*Nacho puts the bag on the loveseat. Silence.*

MARIANA. Hey . . . don't you guys do anything? Don't you work?

NACHO. Yeah, I'm a traveling salesman. I'm out every weekend.

MARIANA. Where?

NACHO. Mar del Plata. I go to Mar del Plata every weekend.

MARIANA. What? You deliver stuff?

NACHO. Yeah, I transport stuff and bring stuff back.

MARIANA. And you go every weekend?

NACHO. Almost every weekend, yeah. Sometimes I don't, sometimes I stay here. And you, what do you do?

MARIANA. Anything and everything. At my last job, the one I just left, I worked at an airport, Ezeiza. Have you been there? I was working there but I quit. I came here with what they paid me, well what they owed me, whatever, I just needed to get the hell out.

NACHO. When your mother was here she said you worked as a . . . what was it, Colo?

COLO. A translator.

NACHO. Yeah, a translator. A translator of English.

MARIANA. Oh, yes, no, but it wasn't as a translator; it was at the airport. You use a lot of English there but I wasn't like a *translator* translator.

COLO. Why did you quit?

MARIANA. I couldn't stand it anymore. I was there for six years. It wasn't a bad job but the whole time you're watching people coming and going, always traveling and you're stuck there in your uniform and all you do is go back and forth between work and home and nothing changes . . . I don't know, I got tired of it. And, besides that, my boyfriend worked there too, okay my ex-boyfriend. It wasn't good for me to see him everyday. So I left. And now I'm just taking it easy. I want a change of scenery, or, I don't know, a change of life. Maybe I should stay here.

**NACHO.** Here.

**MARIANA.** Yes, not here, here. Here on the coast.

**NACHO.** Oh, yeah. Great. It's beautiful here. Peaceful.

**COLO.** Why did you fight?

**MARIANA.** What?

**COLO.** With your boyfriend.

**MARIANA** (*thinking about it for a few seconds*). I don't know, I still don't really understand. I think he stopped loving me, or something like that, but I don't think it was that. I don't know.

**COLO** (*interrupting*). Were you going to go downtown?

**NACHO.** I'm leaving right now.

**COLO.** If not, give me the sweater.

**NACHO.** I'm going now, Colo.

**MARIANA.** I want to play this song for you that I've been listening to. It makes me think about all of this and how to be okay in spite of everything, and how to just live life to its fullest and . . . ciao.

**NACHO.** Is it international?

**MARIANA.** Yeah, I think so, but this one's in Spanish.

**NACHO.** What's it called?

**MARIANA.** "Llévame la vida."[3]

---

**3** "Llévame la vida" is the Spanish version of Robbie Williams' "Better Man," from the album *Sing When You're Winning* (2001).

NACHO. We have a CD player.

MARIANA. Oh, yeah?

*While Mariana and Nacho talk about the song, Colo continues to insist on having the sweater. Nacho comes and goes. The song "Better Man" by Robbie Williams begins to play in Spanish. They sit down on the loveseat listening to it. Mariana is seated between her cousins. She looks devastated. They stay like this. Nacho moves away and Colo kisses her. Nacho doesn't see. Mariana stands up and turns off the music.*

MARIANA. You guys don't have girlfriends.

COLO. No.

NACHO. No.

COLO. Yes he does.

MARIANA. Are you still with . . . what's her name?

NACHO. No.

COLO. Grachi.

MARIANA. Grachi! That's what it was. Are you still seeing her?

COLO. Yes.

NACHO. No, sort of, right now we don't see each other that much.

MARIANA. You two need girlfriends. You don't get enough. Do you fuck?

COLO. I don't need to. I'm fine with how things are. He's the one who's horny.

NACHO. What are you saying?

MARIANA. You don't need to? That's too bad for you. You don't like girls?

NACHO. He takes care of himself.

(OVERLEAF) **FIGURE 1.1** *The Sound It Makes / Algo de ruido hace*, Espacio Callejón, Buenos Aires, 2007. Actor: Esteban Lamothe. *Photograph by Florencia Murno.*

COLO. You shut up. You take care of yourself too, doing whatever you want to that girl. He doesn't like her, he uses her. He does horrible things to her. One day her father is going to catch you and when he catches you, you're going to see just how fast things get ugly . . . He'll take you to the woods . . .

NACHO. What are you saying?

MARIANA. What does he do to her?

NACHO. You'd better think about what you're saying Juan, think about it.

MARIANA. What does he do to her?

NACHO. Juan . . . You don't like to be alone. You're not going to like being alone. He doesn't like to be alone. When I'm off to Mar del Plata he spends the whole weekend riding his bike along the coast. That's if I don't take him. He doesn't like being alone.

COLO. That's not true. I ride my bike because I like it—I like riding my bike. Nacho, you know that I like riding my bike.

NACHO. Yeah, you like it.

MARIANA. What do you do to that girl?

NACHO. Nothing, this is ridiculous.

MARIANA. What does he do, Colo? Aren't you going to tell me?

COLO. He doesn't do anything.

MARIANA. Colo, don't you like girls?

COLO. Yes, I like them.

MARIANA. Then why don't you have a girlfriend? Or boyfriend, or something, I don't know.

COLO. I'm waiting.

MARIANA. What are you waiting for? Love?

COLO. I don't know.

MARIANA. Do you want to fall in love?

*(He doesn't respond. Mariana takes her purse and goes upstairs.)*

I'm sorry but you two are pathetic.

*They follow her with their eyes.*

## II. REGARDING LITERATURE

*The next day. Mariana is seated on the loveseat. She's wearing different clothes. Colo writes. She's finishing a cup of tea as she watches him write. Colo stops and stares at her.*

**COLO.** Mariana, do you remember our grandparents' house in Rumipal . . . and if . . . ? Do you remember if the beds were bunked or side by side?

**MARIANA.** What?

**COLO.** . . . if in Rumipal the beds were bunked or side by side.

**MARIANA.** In which room? The white or the green room? I slept mostly in the green one.

**COLO.** I don't know, the one at the very back.

**MARIANA.** Yeah, the green one.

**COLO.** Yeah.

**MARIANA.** What about it?

**COLO.** . . . if the beds were bunked or side by side.

**MARIANA.** Well, there was a bunk bed, that is, there were two bunks and later they set up a cot that you pulled out from underneath, like a trundle bed. That's when all of us were there and that's where you slept.

**COLO.** Yeah, I slept there. That's why I can't quite . . . I remember this one time Nacho fell from the top bunk and landed on top of me in the middle of the night and it really scared me. But I didn't know, I wasn't sure if I'd dreamt it or what because I was completely asleep. Nacho told me that he thought they'd sawed them in two.

MARIANA. Yeah, no, those were the ones in the other room, the white room. They sawed those in half for our uncles. Isn't that the upstairs room? Isn't that the room I'm sleeping in?

(*Colo stares at her and goes back to writing in his notebook.*)

Yeah, I think so.

*Pause*

MARIANA. Colo, what are you writing about all the time? Are you writing down what I said to you?

COLO. No.

MARIANA. Then what? Is it a diary? Do you write down everything you do?

COLO. No.

*Pause. She moves closer to him.*

MARIANA. Have you always kept a diary or is this something new?

COLO. Always.

MARIANA. What's in it, your thoughts?

COLO. I don't know.

MARIANA. Literature?

COLO. I don't know.

MARIANA. You don't know or you don't want to tell me?

COLO. I don't know.

MARIANA. Why do you want to know about Rumipal?

COLO. So I can record it and remember. Because sometimes when people tell me about it, I know what they're talking about, but then I forget, and then it's as if it had never happened. So I write it down.

MARIANA. Will you show me?

**COLO.** No.

**MARIANA.** Come on Colo, I can help you. I have a very good memory. I remember almost everything. Women have better memories, especially of childhood. Did you know that?

**COLO.** No.

**MARIANA.** Come on, read me something. You slept in the middle because the bunk beds made you claustrophobic. You couldn't stand having anyone on top of you. You didn't like to sleep on the top because it gave you vertigo. That's why you got the cot because there you felt protected and more in control. You were the first to wake up in the morning and you didn't make any noise. You'd sneak out of bed, open the door without a sound, not a bit of sound, and you were off to the woods, off to play. And afterward, much later, around midday, we'd find you sleeping under a tree, or playing by yourself, or doing one thing or another. This happened all the time. We would go to play in the woods and find you asleep there. Aníbal had to be careful not to crush you with the tractor.

**COLO.** Aníbal.

**MARIANA.** He was always careful in the mornings because he knew you might be lying about somewhere, nestled in the branches like a little animal. Like a little animal.

**COLO.** Eucalyptus.

**MARIANA.** What?

**COLO.** The branches were Eucalyptus.

**MARIANA.** Huh. You couldn't learn our names. You could never remember our names so you would invent names for us or you'd give us a nickname: Blondie, Cocoa, Timber, Slim, Giant, Tiny and for him—Brother. You called him "my brother." And you'd ask, "Have you seen my brother?"

**COLO.** My brother.

**MARIANA.** "He went down to the stream with María." And you'd ask, "Which one is María? Giant or Tiny?" "Giant," I'd tell you and you'd run off to find them. You'd go find your brother. And he was always up to something . . .

**COLO.** Nacho.

**MARIANA.** . . . climbing up the highest branch on a tree, discovering caves or secret places, hunting snakes to dissect them, or catching frogs and walking them on a leash until they died. He would take you with him, always making sure you stayed behind him. You stuck to him like glue. "They're so close," Auntie would always say "so close." I don't know why she said that. How strange. "But I trained them to be that way," she would say, and she'd say that you and your brother had to be together always and that she and my mother had raised nice families even though they didn't come from one. That's what she would say to my mother. She was happy. Happy with you both, happy that you weren't apart. Grandmother died and the sisters just withered away, that's what happened. They shut down and withdrew. What happened was that my mother left. Auntie, no, Auntie stayed there. That's what happened, they became depressed. Colo, will you show me?

(*Colo is uncertain. He stares at her transfixed. He finally shakes his head no and goes back to his writing. She moves away, resentful.*)

You guys are still pretty traumatized, aren't you?

(*Colo ignores her.*)

Who found her? Did you find her?

(*Colo stares at her.*)

You found her?

(*Colo stares at her.*)

Juan, do you understand when I speak to you? Was it you who found her?

(*Colo stares at her.*)

What's the problem? Is it the robe?

## IV. TO START AGAIN

*Nacho is standing with a loaf of bread. He stares at Mariana while eating. Mariana is on the loveseat flipping through a magazine.*

NACHO. You sure you don't want some?

MARIANA. I'm sure. I never eat anything in the morning, much less carbs. Too bad you didn't tell me you were going downtown. I have to make a phone call.

NACHO. I thought you were asleep.

MARIANA. No, I've been awake since dawn. That window doesn't have curtains. I didn't come down because I didn't want to disturb you. Why do you both sleep in the living room?

NACHO. It's the only room that gets dark.

MARIANA. Oh. You don't have a telephone here, do you?

NACHO. Yes.

MARIANA. Can I use it?

NACHO. No. The battery's dead.

MARIANA. What do you guys do? You don't need a phone? Don't you need a phone to work?

NACHO. There's a payphone on the main road.

MARIANA. Oh, then I'll go use that one.

NACHO. It doesn't work.

MARIANA. How do you know?

**NACHO.** I just passed by there.

**MARIANA.** I don't believe you. What the hell am I supposed to do? How do you two communicate?

**NACHO.** There's a payphone downtown. If you want, I can take you there later and we can look for apartments while we're out.

**MARIANA.** All right.

(*Silence*)

Hey—can't I sleep down here with you all while I'm here.

**NACHO.** Why?

**MARIANA.** I don't know, I didn't sleep very well last night. I'm not used to sleeping when it's so quiet. And there's too much light. I always sleep with the blinds drawn and closed tight. The moonlight was so bright. It took me forever to fall asleep.

**NACHO.** Did you take that out of the closet?

**MARIANA.** Oh, yes, it was Auntie's, wasn't it? It reminded me of Rumipal. I always admired it. It doesn't bother you that I'm wearing it, does it?

**NACHO.** No.

*Nacho goes to sit on the loveseat.*

**MARIANA.** Just a while ago Colo and I were reminiscing about the green room. Do you remember? He told me that once you fell on top of him in the middle of the night from the top bunk.

**NACHO.** When?

**MARIANA.** I don't know, one time. I don't remember it very well either. He said it happened, but I don't remember it. I think we were all sleeping and you were dreaming and you fell on top of him. He said you almost broke his spine.

**NACHO.** I don't know, I don't remember.

**MARIANA.** He wrote about it in his notebook.

**NACHO.** How do you know?

**MARIANA.** Because he showed it to me.

*Nacho is skeptical of this but isn't sure.*

**NACHO.** And what did it say?

**MARIANA.** I don't know, everything, stuff about when we were kids and some other more recent stuff, too. He never showed it to you?

**NACHO.** No.

**MARIANA.** He never showed it to you?

**NACHO.** No.

**MARIANA.** Are you saying that you never even snuck a peek . . .

**NACHO.** No, he always carries it with him.

**MARIANA.** Ah, so you did want to . . .

**NACHO.** No. . . I mean, just to annoy him. But no.

**MARIANA.** Do you want me to tell you what I saw?

**NACHO.** No.

**MARIANA.** He writes down everything he sees.

**NACHO.** I don't want to know.

**MARIANA.** And he sees much more than you'd think.

**NACHO.** I don't want to know.

**MARIANA.** He knows.

**NACHO.** What?

**MARIANA.** About us. He knows about us.

**NACHO.** What?

**MARIANA.** He says he saw us.

**NACHO.** When?

MARIANA. When we were kids, Ignacio, in Rumipal. When do you think? The last summer we saw each other.

NACHO. What did he see?

MARIANA. Us, Nacho, in the white room.

NACHO. We were alone.

MARIANA. Apparently not.

NACHO. I don't want to know.

MARIANA. You liked me, right? You liked me a lot.

NACHO. I don't know.

MARIANA. I think so. I always loved Colo but more like a brother. But you I've always liked, in a different way. Should we go upstairs for a bit?

NACHO. Upstairs? Really?

MARIANA. Come on, just for a little while.

NACHO. No, I'd better not.

MARIANA. I'm not going to do anything to you. Come on, let's just take a quick nap.

NACHO. Why don't we go into town instead. Didn't you have to make a phone call?

MARIANA. Yes, but we can go later. . . . Let's take a nap and then we'll leave, okay?

NACHO. We could stay here, on the mattresses.

MARIANA. And Colo?

NACHO. He's out biking.

*He's about to give in.*

MARIANA. Are you afraid of going upstairs?

NACHO. Afraid?

MARIANA. Yes, are you afraid? Why don't you go upstairs? Neither of you ever goes upstairs. Why is that?

NACHO. We do go upstairs. When you're not here, we go upstairs. But not now because you're here.

MARIANA. You never go upstairs. I can tell because it's filthy up there.

(*Silence.*)

Are you traumatized, too?

NACHO. What?

MARIANA. I asked you if you were traumatized.

NACHO. No, from what?

MARIANA. I don't know, it just seems like you are. You and your brother are a little weird. A little traumatized. Why don't you sell the house and leave if it still affects you so much.

NACHO. What affects us so much?

MARIANA. I don't know, the house, if it makes you remember.

NACHO. It's our house.

MARIANA. I know, but if it traumatizes you, you should just sell it and be done with it.

NACHO. It doesn't traumatize us. Why would it traumatize us?

MARIANA. I don't know. Why don't you ever go upstairs?

NACHO. But we do.

MARIANA. When was the last time you were upstairs in your mother's room?

NACHO. I don't know.

MARIANA. You don't go upstairs.

NACHO. I do, every now and again.

MARIANA. But when?

**NACHO.** I don't know. Rarely.

**MARIANA.** Never. If everything looks exactly the same.

(*Silence.*)

Did it traumatize you?

**NACHO.** What?

**MARIANA.** What happened to your mother. Did it traumatize you?

**NACHO.** I don't know.

**MARIANA.** Do you want to talk about it?

**NACHO.** No.

**MARIANA.** You might need to.

**NACHO.** I don't know.

**MARIANA.** It was terrible for me. Mama was destroyed.

**NACHO.** No, I don't want to talk about it.

**MARIANA.** But it'll make you feel better. Don't you ever talk about it with Juan?

**NACHO.** About what?

**MARIANA.** I don't know, about your mother, about you.

**NACHO.** No. Yeah, just the normal stuff.

**MARIANA.** What's normal?

**NACHO.** Normal is normal.

**MARIANA.** I think Colo is very traumatized. I actually think you're both not okay.

**NACHO.** Why?

**MARIANA.** I don't know. It just seems that way. It doesn't seem like you're doing very well. I think it might do you good to sell the house. I mean, who knows, but I might think about it.

**NACHO.** Why?

**MARIANA.** I don't know. What do I know? To forget, to start over again.

**NACHO.** Start what?

**MARIANA.** Oh, I don't know, Ignacio. Life.

(*Silence. Nacho is thinking.*)

Don't you want to come with me?

**NACHO.** Where?

**MARIANA.** I don't know. Don't you want to go somewhere together?

**NACHO.** Where to?

**MARIANA.** Wherever you want. I have seven hundred pesos, let's get out of here.

**NACHO.** Like a trip?

**MARIANA.** Yeah, I don't know, let's go somewhere. It's on me.

**NACHO.** And Colo?

**MARIANA.** What about Colo?

**NACHO.** Did you invite him too?

**MARIANA.** No, Nacho . . . I can't invite both of you. Let's go just the two of us, for a couple of days.

**NACHO.** No, I can't. Juan can't be left alone.

**MARIANA.** What do you mean he can't be left alone? How old is he? What do you do when you go to Mar del Plata? Do you bring him?

**NACHO.** He rides his bike around.

**MARIANA.** Oh Nacho, do you really think that you can convince me that he spends his whole weekend riding around on his bike? I don't think so. What does he do when you go to Mar del Plata?

(*Silence.*)

You don't go to Mar del Plata.

(*Nacho doesn't respond. He touches her with a comb. It's strange. She gets up and leaves; she's already on the stairs.*)

You need to go out, at least do something. If not, you're going to turn into crazy old cat people.

NACHO. What?

MARIANA. You know, cat people. People who have a houseful of thousands of cats with cat shit and cat hair everywhere. Super depressed, old cat people. Because now you're still young and kind of attractive. Think about it.

## V. FEEL

*Nacho and Mariana enter and she's wearing different clothes. They're a little too big for her. It's understood that they belonged to her aunt. Mariana and Nacho have spent the whole day together. There is collusion between Mariana and Nacho. Colo is seated in the loveseat.*

MARIANA. I didn't know they had put in a concrete dock . . .

COLO. Where were you?

MARIANA. All over. We were all over. We walked around the town. Nacho showed me a new stretch of boardwalk . . .

NACHO. And the ocean.

MARIANA. We went to the ocean, too. We wanted to see the ocean. It's been so long since I've visited the coast and afterward we went to the little grove, too . . .

NACHO. The woods.

MARIANA. Yes, we went to the woods, too. It was very . . . I don't know . . . it was a little spooky.

COLO. It took you a long time to get back.

MARIANA. And we watched the sunset.

NACHO. What?

COLO. It took you a long time to come back.

NACHO. I don't know, I guess so.

COLO. You told me you'd be an hour and a half, Nacho.

NACHO. We lost track of time.

COLO. You told me an hour and a half.

NACHO. Well, it took a little longer than we thought.

COLO. But you told me an hour and a half.

NACHO. You could have done your own thing.

COLO. I had things to do for an hour and a half but then I was done. I was worried, Nacho.

MARIANA. Oh come on. Colo, it's no big deal. When we were walking home the sun came out and we decided to stop and watch the sunset from the boardwalk. I don't understand what the problem is.

*Silence.*

COLO. I wanted to go, too.

MARIANA. You could have come.

NACHO. You can't leave the house unattended.

MARIANA. Why not?

NACHO. Because someone always has to be here, inside. You know that, Juan.

MARIANA. Why does there always have to be someone here?

COLO. You said an hour and a half, Nacho. You were gone for like four.

MARIANA. Okay, well, what's done is done. Is there anything to eat? I'm starving.

NACHO. There's bread.

MARIANA. Nothing else? Can't we order something?

(*They look at her.*)

Oh right, there's no phone. We should have picked something up while we were out. It didn't even occur to me. Colo, you should go get something.

**NACHO.** Did they patch your tires?

**COLO.** No, I'm not going.

**MARIANA.** Why not? We just got back. Didn't you say you wanted to go out?

**COLO.** Yes, but not alone.

**MARIANA.** Okay, but we just got back.

**COLO.** Will you go with me, Nacho?

**NACHO.** I'm tired.

**COLO.** Come on, Nacho.

**MARIANA.** I don't want to stay here alone.

**NACHO.** Come on, Colo. It'll be a quick trip. With the bike you'll be back in no time.

**COLO.** I don't want to. I'm not hungry. I had some bread.

**MARIANA.** Aw, come on, Colo, it'll just take a second. I come to visit and you don't even offer me a sandwich?

**COLO.** You could have let us know that you were coming.

**MARIANA.** Oh yeah? How? Announce it over the PA system at the resort?

**NACHO.** Okay fine, I'll go. I'm just going to rest for a minute and then I'll go.

**MARIANA.** Okay, I can go with you in a bit. Just not now.

*Uncomfortable silence. Mariana gets up, retrieves a granola bar from her purse, and hums "Better Man." The brothers are sitting on opposite sides of the loveseat. They ignore each other; they're*

FIGURE 1.2 *The Sound It Makes / Algo de ruido hace*, Espacio Callejón, Buenos Aires, 2007. Actors (LEFT TO RIGHT): Esteban Bigliardi, Esteban Lamothe, and Pilar Gamboa. *Photograph by Florencia Murno.*

*incensed. Mariana plays the song "Feel" by Robbie Williams. She dances. At some point the brothers stand up at the same time. Mariana approaches Colo and takes off his sweater. She takes off her aunt's jacket and puts it on Colo. Colo likes it and begins to dance. She applies lipstick to him, and then to Nacho. The three of them continue dancing. It starts to get a little violent. Nacho grabs her from behind and restrains her. He offers her to Colo. Colo approaches her and kisses her clumsily, excitedly; he touches her. She gets away and sits on the loveseat. She's disturbed. The next song by Robbie Williams begins to play. They stand there looking at each other. They look at her. Finally, Colo goes upstairs. Nacho watches*

*him go. He looks at her. He follows his brother. She doesn't move.
She grabs her CD and her purse in a rush; she exits hurriedly
through the door. The space remains empty for a couple of seconds.
At the same time, you can hear the brothers moving around upstairs.
Mariana bursts in like a gust of wind. She has nowhere to go. She's
upset. She sits in the loveseat and lights a cigarette. Colo comes
downstairs. He is changed, more radiant, one might say, but also
more intense. Disheveled. He sits on the other side of the loveseat.
Mariana is a little ill at ease and she moves to sit on the back of the
loveseat. . . . Silence. Colo picks up his notebook and begins to read.*

COLO. She was bathed in white light. And lovely . . . her face luminous,
turned toward the light, her lips bright red. That's how I saw her.
She possessed a stillness I've never witnessed before. Complete
stillness. Nothing alive is that still, not even while sleeping. Hers
was a stillness that doesn't exist in this world . . . in the living
world. And it was her but it wasn't. Something had left. It was no
longer there. I think I woke up from the absence of sound, because
something alive makes sound, it makes a sound, even if imper-
ceptible, there's a sound. I woke up because there was silence. The
emptiness woke me. That's when I saw the sun shining on her face,
she was motionless. She didn't want to move. She couldn't. I kept
looking at her. I didn't want to touch her at first. I was afraid
because it was unfamiliar, different. It wasn't her anymore, she
wasn't my mother. She was something else, she was already something else. I watched her, I watched her for a long time until I got
used to her, how she was, her new way of being, how she was going
to be from now on, and that's when I touched her. I touched her
hand, just her hand, and it was cold . . . So cold and still. The air
was warm but she was cold, and still. Her hand was heavy. I held
it in mine and after a while I kissed her cheek. Her scent was gone.

I said goodbye, Mother. I love you, I'm always going to love you silently. And I came downstairs. And I sat here. This is where I sat. *Nacho comes downstairs during Colo's monologue. He is also disheveled.*

**NACHO.** Until I came.

**COLO.** Until Nacho came from Mar del Plata.

**MARIANA.** You stayed the whole weekend sitting here with my aunt . . . upstairs?

**COLO.** Just one day.

**NACHO.** I got here the next day.

**MARIANA.** I couldn't come.

**COLO.** You could have at least called.

**MARIANA.** I couldn't.

**NACHO.** You were the only one of the Furlongs that wasn't here.

**MARIANA.** I couldn't. I'm sorry. I already told you, it was a strange time. That's why I came now. I wanted to see you both.

**COLO.** It's late.

**NACHO.** Yes, it's late.

**MARIANA.** I couldn't, I couldn't bear it.

**NACHO.** It doesn't matter. Still, we don't love you anymore.

**MARIANA.** What?

**COLO.** I said we don't love you anymore. As a cousin.

**NACHO.** We don't love you anymore.

**MARIANA.** What do you mean you don't love me?

**COLO.** We don't love you anymore. It's over.

(OVERLEAF) **FIGURE 1.3** *The Sound It Makes / Algo de ruido hace*, Espacio Callejón, Buenos Aires, 2007. Actors (LEFT TO RIGHT): Pilar Gamboa, Esteban Bigliardi, and Esteban Lamothe. *Photograph by Florencia Murno.*

**MARIANA.** What's over? You can't stop loving me. It's not something you decide.

**COLO.** It was a slow process.

**NACHO.** It was gradual. We stopped loving you.

**COLO.** Bit by bit.

**NACHO.** And now we don't love you.

**MARIANA.** What you're saying is horrible.

**COLO.** No.

**NACHO.** It isn't horrible. It's the truth. But you can still stay if you want.

**MARIANA.** Where?

**NACHO.** Here, you can stay here if you want. For a few days. Until you find something.

**MARIANA.** I don't know if I want to stay.

(*They look at her. Silence. Mariana becomes distraught.*)

You're my cousins.

**NACHO.** Yes.

**COLO.** Yes.

**MARIANA.** You can't stop being my cousins.

**COLO.** We are your cousins.

**NACHO.** But we don't love you as cousins. That love is gone.

**MARIANA.** So what am I now?

**NACHO.** A cousin.

**MARIANA.** But you don't love me?

**COLO.** No.

**MARIANA.** And you can't love me again?

*They look at each other.*

**NACHO.** How?

MARIANA. I don't know. What if I do something for you. If I stay, if I take care of you.

COLO. What for?

MARIANA. I don't know. So that you get better, so that you go back to loving me again.

*They remain silent. They keep thinking. Colo takes his notebook and starts to read.*

COLO. No. When we were together, I saw you with my brother in the white room. You were kissing.

MARIANA. When were we boyfriend and girlfriend?

(*He looks at the notebook.*)

Are you talking about Rumipal? That was twenty years ago, Colo.

NACHO. Were you together?

COLO. Yes.

MARIANA. No, we weren't together. We pretended we were once but we were just playing around. We weren't boyfriend and girlfriend, Juan.

COLO. You kissed him. And you wanted to leave together. You wanted to take him with you.

MARIANA. Where?

COLO. I don't know. You invited him out. With the seven hundred pesos.

MARIANA. That's now. You're mixing everything up, Colo. You're mixing everything up.

NACHO. I wasn't going to go.

COLO. I know.

MARIANA. What do you mean you weren't going to go? You're the one who suggested that we go somewhere, that we should start over again.

**COLO.** Start what?

**MARIANA.** I don't know, life.

**COLO.** Life doesn't start over.

**MARIANA.** I know! That's exactly what I told him!

**NACHO.** You can't start over.

**MARIANA.** What are you saying to me? I'm the one who said that!

**COLO.** I think you're going to have to go.

**MARIANA.** And where do you want me to go?

**NACHO.** I don't know, but you can't stay here.

**MARIANA.** So, what, you're going to throw me out on the street?

**COLO.** You have seven hundred pesos.

**MARIANA.** What does that have to do with anything? You're just going to throw me out in the middle of the night?

*They look at each other. They're thinking.*

**NACHO.** If not, you can sleep here with us. Tonight.

**MARIANA.** Where?

**NACHO.** Here, with us. And tomorrow you leave. Where would you go now anyway?

## VI. THE INTRUDER

*Colo tells the short story "The Intruder" by Jorge Luis Borges to Nacho. Mariana is under the sheet.*

**COLO.** They were also two brothers. English, or something like that. Blond, I think, or redheads. I'm not sure. I always imagined them with freckles.

**NACHO.** Blond.

COLO. Let's say blond. And they were very close and lived together on

COLO. Let's say blond. And they were very close and lived together on
a farm or a ranch or maybe something not that big. Maybe it was
just a big house in a town.

NACHO. A big house.

COLO. Yeah, a big house and the two of them lived there alone. And
they got along very well, or that's what they said. Or, I'm not really
sure because they were always very close, always together those
two.

(*Nacho sits down. He wants more information.*)

Well, one day one of them, I'm not sure which one, I think the
oldest one, he brings a woman home to live with them. She's like
a girlfriend but he also uses her like a maid. Or he was going to
use her, because that's the kind of person he was.

NACHO. Pretty?

COLO. I think so. Yes, it said she was, or at least for that neighborhood
she was pretty. For that neighborhood she was considered pretty.

NACHO. And did he love her?

COLO. I don't think so. I don't think that it said whether or not he loved
her. I'm not sure if he was the loving type. He was very ill-tem-
pered. But the younger brother, yes. I'm sure she loved the younger
brother. What happened was that the brother, the younger brother,
he started to misbehave, getting drunk all the time and he kind of
lost it for a while.

NACHO. Because of the girl.

COLO. Yes, because of the girl.

NACHO. He fell in love.

COLO. It seems like it. He fell in love with his brother's girlfriend. And
so the older brother, who loves his younger brother very much,

FIGURE 1.4 *The Sound It Makes / Algo de ruido hace*, Espacio Callejón, Buenos Aires, 2007. Actors (LEFT TO RIGHT): Esteban Bigliardi, Pilar Gamboa, and Esteban Lamothe. *Photograph by Florencia Murno.*

one night tells him: "she's all yours, use her if you want." He says something like that.

**NACHO.** He said, "use her"?

**COLO.** I don't remember exactly, but that was the idea, to "use her."

**NACHO.** But did he use those exact words or say something else?

**COLO.** I don't know, Nacho. I don't remember. So, anyway, the other one falls in love.

**NACHO.** The brother.

**COLO.** Yes, the other brother, the younger one.

**NACHO.** The younger one. He was already in love.

**COLO.** Yes, but he falls even more in love. And that's when they begin to share her. They don't say anything about it but they share her.

**NACHO.** And the girl?

**COLO.** What about her?

**NACHO.** What does she say?

**COLO.** I don't know. She doesn't say a word. It doesn't say anything about her. The brothers don't say anything about the girl but it starts to change them. They fight all the time about little things.

**NACHO.** They're both in love.

**COLO.** They're jealous. And they come up with a plan. They talk about it one day and decide to go through with it. They make her pack up her clothes and they take her to a town far away where they sell her to a brothel.

**NACHO.** And they leave her there?

**COLO.** Yeah, they sell her. Well, it seemed like everything was over but it turns out that they were both still secretly visiting her. The youngest one was the most in love. And his brother knew it. So one day they run into each other there, at the brothel, so the older brother tells the younger brother they should bring her back, that it didn't make any sense to leave her there, that it was better to keep her close. So they go get her. . . . And they go back to living together just the three of them. And one day, I think it was a Sunday or Saturday, I'm not sure but it was the weekend, the youngest was out and when he returns his brother tells him to come with him to run an errand, so they get in the wagon or what-ever it is that they have . . .

**NACHO.** A wagon?

COLO. Yeah, I don't know, one of those things attached to a horse. A wagon. Anyway, he tells him to come with him because he needs help carrying something. They carry the sack and go to a clearing far away from everything in the middle of the woods, and it's already dark and that's when he tells his younger brother to help him dig a grave for the girl because he had killed her.

NACHO. The older brother.

COLO. Yes, the older one got tired of it and he killed her when the younger one was out and now they have to bury her secretly with all of her things, so that she doesn't bother them anymore, and they hug each other and begin to cry.

NACHO. They cried?

COLO. Yes, I think it said they cried. Or at least that's the image I have. But they definitely hug. I'm sure they hug.

NACHO. They kill her because they love her.

COLO. Yeah, no. I don't know. Because she couldn't belong to both of them. He killed her for them, so they could go back to the way things were. The story is about the brothers.

NACHO. But they ended up alone.

COLO. Yeah, well, I don't know, they had each other. I think that was enough. Do you understand?

NACHO. I don't know.

COLO. Well, I don't know either, I'm just telling you what the story said.

THE END

THE WHOLE OF TIME

The Whole of Time premiered at Espacio Callejón in Buenos Aires in 2009. The play was directed by Romina Paula with assistant direction by Leandro Orellano, set design by Alicia Leloutre and Matías Sendón, and lighting by Matías Sendón.

## CAST

| | |
|---:|:---|
| **ANTONIA** | Pilar Gamboa |
| **LORENZO** | Esteban Bigliardi |
| **URSULA** | Susana Pampín |
| **MAXIMILIANO** | Esteban Lamothe |

TRANSLATED BY **Jean Graham-Jones**

"A poet's vocation is something that rests on something as thin
and fine as the web of a spider. [ . . . ] Few, very few are able to
do it alone! Great help is needed! I *did* give it! She *didn't*."
                                    —Mrs. Venable in *Suddenly Last Summer*[1]

"Anyone who thinks hard about the nature of time will understand that what it takes to bring something into existence is also
needed to keep it in existence at each Moment of its duration."

                                                            —René Descartes[2]

*Antonia and Lorenzo are at home, listening to "No hay nada más difícil
que vivir sin ti" (Also known as "Si no te hubieras ido" / "There's nothing
more difficult than living without you" [1983]) by Mexican singer-
songwriter Marco Antonio Solís.*

**ANTONIA.** He writes her this song from jail. What's funny is that it
    sounds like a love song, a song about being apart. But what's really
    going on is that she's already dead. And she's dead because he
    killed her, the singer-songwriter killed her.

**LORENZO.** That's true?

**ANTONIA.** Yeah, everyone knows that. It's just something you know.

---

1 Tenessee Williams, *Suddenly Last Summer* [1958] (New York: Dramatists Play
Service, 1986), p. 36.

2 René Descartes, *Meditations on First Philosophy: With Selections from Objections
and Replies* [1639] (John Cottingham ed. and trans.), 2ND EDN (Cambridge: Cambridge
University Press, 2013), p. 39.

**LORENZO.** But did he go to prison for murder?

**ANTONIA.** What do you think? He killed a woman. His own woman.

**LORENZO.** How did he kill her?

**ANTONIA.** I don't know exactly. I'd say he stabbed her with a knife. There was blood, I remember that. It could have been a knifing.

**LORENZO.** Or gunshots.

**ANTONIA.** Yes, no, that's from a distance, it's more cowardly. Less passionate. Knifings are more passionate.

**LORENZO.** Stabbing.

**ANTONIA.** Yeah, but I'm not sure.

**LORENZO.** But was the guy a murderer and famous?

**ANTONIA.** Really famous, he's a star, what does that have to do with it? He's a singer-songwriter who became famous as a singer-songwriter. Mexicans are like that, passionate.

**LORENZO.** And what does that have to do with it?

**ANTONIA.** We kill our women if they betray us And it's not seen as bad. On the contrary. It's what real macho men do.

*Antonia shoots with her fingers while Lorenzo changes his shoes.*

**LORENZO.** Go on, Pun,[3] keep going, this is interesting.

(*Little gunshots.*)

If I have to get up, you're gonna pay.

*Antonia keeps on shooting, provoking Lorenzo, who gets up and jumps on top of her. She pulls away, laughing.*

**ANTONIA.** No, seriously, Pun, the guy kills his woman, he writes her a song out of spite and becomes a famous multimillionaire. His

---

3 Antonia and Lorenzo call each other "Pun" or "Puni" (pronounced *poon*, *poony*), a secret sibling code of affection. Antonia calls their mother "Uschi" (pronounced *ooschi*). [Trans.]

audience loves him and forgives him. Just look at how those women stare at him in his concerts. The men too, everybody's captivated, enthralled like they've been hypnotized. You can tell it's really powerful stuff being produced.

**LORENZO.** I didn't know about the crime. I always thought it was a love song.

**ANTONIA.** Because it is a love song.

**LORENZO.** In what way?

**ANTONIA.** The only way. It's about love. Killing her doesn't mean he doesn't love her, that he didn't love her. On the contrary. It's only that it's a very passionate, out-of-control kind of love.

**LORENZO.** A Mexican love.

**ANTONIA.** Exactly. But not because it's macho. Because of the sense of humor, maybe. Probably in Mexico people forgive or tolerate somebody killing his wife and then selling millions of records where he sings to the dead woman he misses so much. It's a question of distance, distancing, getting past it. A sense of humor. It's looking at it humorously.

**LORENZO.** Maybe.

**ANTONIA.** Like the Frida painting with all the little nips, Pun.

**LORENZO.** The one with the hair?

**ANTONIA.** "Look, if I loved you it was because of your hair. Now that you're bald, I don't love you anymore."[4] You're talking about the one with her hair chopped off, nope, that's not the one.

**LORENZO.** It's not? Then I don't know which one you're talking about, which one was the little nips one? I don't have them all memorized.

---

4 At the top of Frida Kahlo's *Self-Portrait with Cropped Hair* [*Autorretrato con el pelo cortado*], the artist painted the lyrics from a Mexican folk song: "Mira que si te quise fué por el pelo, Ahora que estás pelona, ya no te quiero." [Trans.]

ANTONIA. Yeah, Pun, the one with the murderer. "A Few Small Nips!"[5], just like that, with an exclamation mark at the end.

LORENZO. I don't remember, I don't have them all memorized.

ANTONIA. It has the title at the top. There's a man standing behind a bed where there's a woman who's been stabbed, everything's suspended in the middle of the room. There's the bed and on the bed there's a naked woman who's been stabbed and is all bloody, and behind her and the bed there's a man standing holding a knife. He's completely dressed, I think he's wearing black or dark brown pants and a white shirt, also bloody. And at the top two little birds are holding up a little banner that says: "A Few Small Nips!"

LORENZO. Nope, don't know it, I don't remember, I don't have them all memorized.

*Lorenzo shows his sister a sweater.*

ANTONIA. With that shirt?

LORENZO. Yeah.

ANTONIA. No way. What, you're leaving now?

LORENZO. No, in a bit.

ANTONIA. So, can you see it's Mexican? This is a real-life case of a guy who stabs his wife I don't know how many hundreds of times and when the police pick him up, he says he only gave her a couple of little nips . . . That's what was in the papers and that's why Frida painted it.

LORENZO. And those things don't happen here?

ANTONIA. What?

LORENZO. I don't know. I was thinking that here we also have million-aire singer-songwriter murderers or men like that little nips-guy. Or Fridas.

---

**5** In the original, "Unos cuantos piquetitos." [Trans.]

ANTONIA. Not like that. I think it's a different sense of humor.

LORENZO. Like none.

ANTONIA. I wouldn't say none, but it's more acidic, right? Or silent. Like Barreda,[6] for example, or Pantriste.[7]

LORENZO. Which one was Pantriste?

ANTONIA. The kid that killed his buddies because they called him "Pantriste, Pantriste." Always silent, silent, silent, until one day bang! And there you go. But in cases like that it was guns. A gun is something else, it's like you don't want to get your hands dirty: you hold the other guy in such low esteem that you don't even want to touch him, you don't want to have anything to do with his blood. That's clearly more of a gun thing. But then, every so often, you'll find 113 stab wounds or something like that, but it's more isolated. So I'd say. The tendency here is more toward guns, right?

LORENZO. What do I know.

ANTONIA. Do you think of yourself as more of a gunslinger or a knife-fighter?

LORENZO. Guns.

ANTONIA. Totally. Because you're a sissy. You wouldn't lay your hands on somebody even if they beat the shit out of you.

LORENZO. No. You? Which would you choose? I don't remember.

ANTONIA. I think both.

---

6 Ricardo Alberto Barreda (b. 1936) is a retired odontologist who in 1992 killed his wife, his two adult daughters, and his mother-in-law. Barreda entered the popular imagination as the image of feminicide, but he has also appeared as popular devotional figure San Barreda, patron saint of misogyny. [Trans.]

7 "Pantriste" [Sad Bread] is the cartoon-character nickname given to Javier Romero, who in 2000 at the age of nineteen took his mother's gun and shot thirteen classmates, killing three, as they were leaving school, saying "I'm going to be respected." [Trans.]

**LORENZO.** Pepita the Pistol-Packer.[8]

**ANTONIA.** Or Antonia the Butcher-Girl. Yeah, I figure both. A gun if I don't care about you, a blade if I think you're cute.

*Antonia pretends to take a knife stab in her chest. Lorenzo looks at her but doesn't know what to do.*

**LORENZO.** Did you talk to Mom?

**ANTONIA.** Hey, hold on a little.

**LORENZO.** What's the matter?

**ANTONIA.** Hold on a bit.

*Antonia breathes with difficulty. She walks over to the bench and sits down next to her brother. She appears to be getting sick.*

**LORENZO.** Do you want me to call Mom?

*Antonia lets loose a big laugh and suddenly she's back to normal. Her brother yanks her hair.*

**ANTONIA.** Not my hair!

(*Antonia goes back to her desk.*)

Yeah, right, definitely a gunslinger . . . "Do you want me to call Mom?"

**LORENZO.** Smart-ass!

*After a while, Antonia's sitting at the computer.*

**ANTONIA.** So where are you going?

**LORENZO.** They're coming by in a while to pick me up.

**ANTONIA.** But where are you going?

**LORENZO.** They're coming by in a while to pick me up.

---

8 *La historia casi verdadera de Pepita la Pistolera* [The almost true history of Pepita the Pistol-Packer] is a 1993 Uruguayan fictional film based on the true story of a middle-aged woman who committed a series of credit-office robberies in Montevideo using a "gun" that was discovered later to have been an umbrella handle. [Trans.]

ANTONIA. Are you in the mood for a story?

(*Lorenzo shakes his head no.*)

Title: "Accident survivors." Two brothers. You have an older brother. Both have girlfriends. I'm the older brother's girlfriend. The four of us do a lot of things together, we all get along great. You, the brothers, are dazzlingly handsome. We're all in love, us with you, you with us.

LORENZO. Sounds good.

ANTONIA. One night your brother takes your girlfriend to the station. It's late and you two don't want her to walk by herself, so your brother offers to take her in his car.

FIGURE 2.1 *The Whole of Time / El tiempo todo entero*, Espacio Callejón, Buenos Aires, September 2012. Actors (LEFT TO RIGHT): Esteban Bigliardi and Pilar Gamboa. *Photograph by Sebastián Arpesella.*

LORENZO. And where are we, you and me?

ANTONIA. I stayed here at home, studying, and you stayed at your place. You didn't go in the car because your brother was going to drop her off on his way.

LORENZO. And then?

ANTONIA. They have a wreck. They have a wreck and they both die.

LORENZO. The two that aren't us.

ANTONIA. Exactly.

LORENZO. That's terrible. What about us?

ANTONIA. We're destroyed. Destroyed and united by this terrible tragedy. We see each other all the time, because nobody else understands us better than we do, since we share this pain. We see each other all the time. You remind me so much of my true love. You look like him so much . . . One night I go to see you at your place, like I have on so many other nights, and we're listening to music, and we're laughing, and everything's very confusing. That's it.

LORENZO. How much older are you than me?

ANTONIA. Four years.

LORENZO. And how old am I?

ANTONIA. That doesn't matter.

LORENZO. How much time has passed since the accident?

ANTONIA. Months.

LORENZO. Let me think about it. Negative. No.

ANTONIA. Not even one confused kiss? I'm really cute. And I'm really torn up. Just like you. And your brother loved me.

LORENZO. But my heart is completely broken and it doesn't even occur to me to start over.

ANTONIA. But it's not about starting over, it's about getting confused.

**LORENZO.** Even more reason. Besides, I'd ask us not to see each other again.

**ANTONIA.** Really? That's harsh.

**LORENZO.** I'd do it to forget and so you can move on. Because if you don't, with that look-alike thing you can end up stuck your whole life. I'm kicking you out so you can pull yourself together.

**ANTONIA.** So I do matter to you.

**LORENZO.** Of course, you matter to me, you were my brother's true love, how are you not going to matter to me.

**ANTONIA.** But you don't love me.

**LORENZO.** Exactly.

**ANTONIA.** And if I insist? If I convince you?

*Antonia propositions him, she pounces on him, tries to kiss him.*

**LORENZO.** Stop, you're being gross.

**ANTONIA.** Kiss me, kiss me.

**LORENZO.** Enough, Puni, get out. Code red, Antonia, code red!

*Ursula enters, sees them and tries to separate them.*

**URSULA.** You're going to get hurt. Antonia! Get out of here. Did you hear me?

(*Antonia exits, taking an ironic bow.*)

Did you talk to your sister?

**LORENZO.** Yes.

**URSULA.** Did you talk? What did she say?

**LORENZO.** About what?

**URSULA.** About your leaving, about your wanting to leave.

**LORENZO.** Um, no, I didn't talk about that.

**URSULA.** When are you thinking of telling her?

**LORENZO.** Telling her what?

URSULA. That you're leaving, Lorenzo, that, nothing more or less.

LORENZO. It's not for sure. When I know for sure, I'll tell her.

URSULA. But why don't you begin preparing her?

LORENZO. Preparing her for what?

URSULA. For when you're not here.

LORENZO. Do you ever think about what you're saying? Are you paying attention to yourself? Exactly how do you imagine it works—preparing somebody for something? Worse, preparing somebody for something completely uncertain, where not even you are going to be around, because that's what this is about, you're not going to be here, you're not going to be around.

URSULA. Brilliant. Are you done? I'm saying that you should talk to her about your desire to go live somewhere else, even if you're not sure yet.

LORENZO. Why?

URSULA. What kind of relationship do you two have if you don't? You have a lovely relationship, so I don't understand why you'd want to hide from her something so important to you.

LORENZO. I'm not hiding it from her. I'm waiting for the right moment to tell her.

URSULA. Now.

LORENZO. No, I can't do it now.

URSULA. Why not?

LORENZO. Because I can't do it now.

URSULA. Why not?

LORENZO. Because I can't.

*Lorenzo shows her the book he's reading.*

URSULA. So when do you think you'll tell her?

**LORENZO.** Later.

**URSULA.** Later like two in the morning?

**LORENZO.** Maybe.

*Ursula snatches the book from him and moves away.*

**URSULA.** Do it today. If you don't tell her yourself, I'll do it.

**LORENZO.** Don't even think about it.

**URSULA.** Silence can do a lot of damage, Lorenzo. Not knowing can hurt.

**LORENZO.** I don't know if I agree with that. Sometimes the truth is, I prefer not to know. It seems to me that sometimes not saying things can be an act of kindness too, of care. I'd say that the great percentage of all the things I know about you, if you'd given me the chance to choose, I'd prefer never to have heard them.

*Ursula throws the book at her son. Lorenzo takes the hit. He picks up the book, looks at it, goes over to his mother and balances it on her chest.*

**LORENZO.** The next time I'll throw it back.

*Lorenzo takes his book and moves away. Antonia comes in and sits back down at the computer. Úrsula has a belt buckle in her hand.*

**URSULA.** Antonia . . .

**ANTONIA.** What?

**URSULA.** Do you like this?

**ANTONIA.** Yes, very pretty.

**URSULA.** I bought it for myself today. You can borrow it whenever you want.

**ANTONIA.** Not my style, thanks.

**URSULA.** But just ask me if you want to borrow it.

**ANTONIA.** Whatever.

(*Ursula begins to hum a song, walks around the room, goes over to the stereo. She pushes a few buttons, the sound comes on at full volume but out of tune.*)

[*in English*] "Play!"

URSULA. You don't say. It says [*in English*] "reading, reading"—it's reading.

(*Chavela Vargas's "Macorina" begins to play. Ursula goes over to her daughter and tries to get her to dance. At first Antonia declines but then finally accepts. They do a few varied steps. At some point Antonia gets over her embarrassment and begins to lead, as if she were the man. Ursula lets herself be led. Antonia breaks away and goes back to the computer. Her mother, like a wounded boyfriend, spitefully turns off the music.*)

Moody girl.

(*Ursula walks around the room.*)

I'm not talking about a traditional relationship but something, some type of relationship. Something more your style.

ANTONIA. This again?

URSULA. That's all I'm going to say, I'm not saying anything more.

*Antonia thinks about it.*

ANTONIA. It's like you're giving me a pink skirt and then insisting I wear it. It's almost offensive, Uschi.

URSULA. Don't call me Uschi.

ANTONIA. Don't tell me "to get a boyfriend."

URSULA. I didn't say that. I didn't say boyfriend. I said something, some type, whatever you want.

ANTONIA. That's worse.

URSULA. Okay, enough, I already said I'm sorry, I'm not going to say anything else. Look, my lips are sealed, moving on.

*Antonia's still thinking. She doesn't let it go.*    **55**

THE WHOLE OF TIME

**ANTONIA.** And besides, it's violent, because you're disregarding what I'm expressing, what I'm trying or attempting to express through my behavior.

**URSULA.** So what is it you're expressing?

**ANTONIA.** Who I am, this is who I am. Do I look so bad to you?

(*Ursula doesn't respond.*)

Do I look bad to you?

**URSULA.** No, honey.

**ANTONIA.** It depends on where you're coming from you mean to say.

**URSULA.** No, darling, Antonia, I don't think you look bad. You're lovely, look at what you are.

**ANTONIA.** It depends on what you're hoping for. And you're right, it's a question of points of view or expectations. The thing is I like being here and I choose not to go out so I can have the bonds that I have with you two and develop those. Plus the people I get to know right here.

**URSULA.** Your broadband friends.

**ANTONIA.** The broadband is a service, Mom. Are you leaving now?

**URSULA.** They're coming by in a bit to pick me up.

**ANTONIA.** Now if there's something, for example, I can't understand at all is that need, that drive people have to leave. Like traveling? The majority go, look, and come back. That's traveling?

**URSULA.** I guess so.

**ANTONIA.** I don't get it, I swear I don't get it. Because it's not that I'm in denial or that I'm stubborn. I am stubborn, but I mean to say that I give them a chance, I give myself a chance, I think, I reflect, consider other options, and I've never been able to understand going far away, deep down I just don't get it.

**URSULA.** Well, people travel to . . . experience. See things they haven't seen before.

**ANTONIA.** Why?

**URSULA.** To see them, to . . . experience them.

**ANTONIA.** You already said that, but what does it mean to experience? See something for five minutes or a half hour, a day, a whole week, that's experiencing?

**URSULA.** Well, I don't know.

**ANTONIA.** You don't know, because that's not experiencing, that's seeing. Experiencing is making it your own. I don't need to see something live in order to experience it, I'd rather imagine it. I even think the bond is that much deeper if you give attributes to things, attributes that you've imagined, that are a combination of something from Object X—the Trevi Fountain, for example—and your imagination. Or even better: a combination of the fountain, what they've told you about the fountain, what you saw of the fountain in some movie, and your imagination. And something you might have read, some description of the fountain in some novel.

**URSULA.** I don't know, I like seeing . . . going somewhere, getting impressions.

**ANTONIA.** Well, you don't travel all that much yourself.

**URSULA.** Not now, because you two are here. But with your father we loved to travel when we were young. We'd always be running away someplace for a couple of days, even if it was nearby, up to the delta[9] or to go camping.

**ANTONIA.** To play caveman.

---

9 Tigre is a town located on an island on the Paraná Delta, about 17 miles north of Buenos Aires. Tigre also refers to the delta's many islands, which are a common weekend destination. [Trans.]

URSULA. To be in nature. You go a couple of miles away and you're in the middle of nowhere.

ANTONIA. So the bugs can get you.

URSULA. To see the stars, the sky, smell the grass, bathe in a stream, be alone in nature.

ANTONIA. So the bugs can get you and you can't get clean and you eat bad and miss all the basics of life. No thanks, that doesn't interest me. Besides, we weren't talking about life out in nature, we were talking about experiencing. So you spend a week in the delta, does that mean you've experienced the delta?

URSULA. More than if you never went.

ANTONIA. That's different. I'd rather you told me about it. Besides, there's a lot of humidity and mosquitos in the delta. You're stuck on some island, you can't get away. And if you want to go for a walk, you have to go around in a circle. It's terrible.

URSULA. I'm not trying to sell you anything.

ANTONIA. Yeah, you are, a boyfriend.

URSULA. I just don't want you to end up alone, Antonia.

ANTONIA. You're both here.

URSULA. But we're family.

ANTONIA. Exactly.

URSULA. I'm talking about a companion, somebody you can share your life with.

ANTONIA. Like you.

URSULA. . . .

ANTONIA. Like you and your companion.

URSULA. Well, I had one, for many years. And I have one now, even though it's different . . . And anyway, I have you two.

**ANTONIA.** Exactly.

**URSULA.** Exactly what?

**ANTONIA.** We have each other. If you have me and I get a, I don't know, a companion, you don't have me anymore. It doesn't add up, it doesn't make sense, Uschi.

**URSULA.** Did I make you be like this?

**ANTONIA.** No, I did it all by myself.

(*She thinks.*)

A little bit of each.

**URSULA.** I like you the way you are, I adore you, you're the most special person I know, really, you're my favorite person . . . Next to your brother, of course. What I'm saying and this is the last thing I'm going to say is that it hurts me you don't know more people, that you don't give yourself the chance to meet more people and experience more things, that's all. I'll shut up.

*Antonia, resigned, says something that she must have said an infinite number of times.*

**ANTONIA.** It's not a question of quantity.

**URSULA.** Silent. As the grave.

**ANTONIA.** Please.

*Lorenzo appears with a book in his hand. Ursula changes in front of her children as she gets ready to leave.*

**LORENZO.** Are you going to get married?

**URSULA.** Who?

**LORENZO.** You and your boyfriend.

**URSULA.** I don't have a boyfriend.

**LORENZO.** So who are you going out with?

**URSULA.** With a friend. Augusto. You've both met him.

LORENZO. But you'd like it.

URSULA. What.

LORENZO. If he asked you to marry him.

URSULA. No way! Augusto is a lovely guy, but he's just a friend.

LORENZO. But he could stop being one.

URSULA. But no.

ANTONIA. Why not?

URSULA. Because that's that, because I already did that, now I prefer to have friends, it's a lot cheaper.

ANTONIA. Cheaper?

URSULA. Economically. A lot less work. It's like love but less complex. Purer.

ANTONIA. So I'm right.

URSULA. No. I'm talking about this moment in my life. And having gone through a different one. I don't regret having been there.

LORENZO. Where? What did I miss?

ANTONIA. Companion-land.

URSULA. I loved and was loved. I fell in love, I fell out of love, I went through sickness, uprooting, death . . . I had my children, I had them. I went through reconciliations . . . Yes, sir, I even lived through getting back together. I didn't miss a thing.

ANTONIA. Us.

URSULA. But that's my life. This one.

ANTONIA. Ours, too.

URSULA. Yes, but no. These types of experiences are non-transferable. You both have to make your own path.

ANTONIA. No, thanks. You think that I can't feel spite, I can't breathe it?

LORENZO. Pun.

ANTONIA. What? We're chatting.

URSULA. I don't regret a thing, daughter.

ANTONIA. No, something was missing.

URSULA. What are you trying to say?

ANTONIA. It's good that you don't have any regrets. Because if on top of all that horrible stuff you had to go through, you cursed yourself over something you did . . .

URSULA. It's not "horrible," honey, that's life.

LORENZO. It takes all sorts to make a world.

URSULA. Exactly, it takes all sorts. Did I pass all this fear on to you? That's what hurts me, you see? I would have regrets about that.

ANTONIA. What fear? I'm not afraid, enough with that.

LORENZO. I think she looks strong.

ANTONIA. I already know that, because I am strong.

URSULA. But you're always raw, Antonia.

ANTONIA. Raw? That's just another cliché, a prejudice. If I'm raw, then you've suffered a lot and you're suffering all the time and you're broken.

URSULA. Broken? What do you mean broken? What's this, something new?

LORENZO. Stop it, nobody's suffering here, we're like this, I think you're both fine, only you just get each other all wound up. Things aren't that complicated. You're beautiful, Mom. Don't put any more makeup on, it makes you look older.

ANTONIA. I don't understand makeup. It seems so ugly to me.

URSULA. Thanks, son. You're being sour, Antonia, I don't like you when you get like this.

LORENZO. Let's have a drink, let's have a brother-and-sister night.

**URSULA.** Don't wait up for me, I'll be late.

**LORENZO.** Will he bring you home?

**URSULA.** Yes, but don't wait up, I'll be late. Take advantage of the chance to talk . . .

(*Antonia and Lorenzo look at her, without moving.*)

Am I a pretty mama?

**LORENZO.** Yes.

**ANTONIA.** Yes.

*Antonia nods, almost in spite of herself, but she can't say the word. She could almost cry from the pain. But she's not going to.*

**URSULA.** Love me?

(*Antonia and Lorenzo nod in agreement.*)

Do you love me?

*Lorenzo nods his head. Ursula goes over to her son and kisses him on the mouth. She then moves her head close to Antonia's and is just about to kiss her but doesn't do it. She leaves. Lorenzo goes over to his sister to hug her. Antonia doesn't want him to and pushes him away. Lorenzo hugs her anyway, she quits resisting. Maximiliano enters. He sees the embrace and interrupts it. He whistles a greeting.*

**LORENZO.** This is Maxi, Maximiliano, from the grill.

*Antonia goes over to the computer, moving away to regain her composure but not leaving. The friends greet each other.*

**MAXIMILIANO.** Some place, Ace! Yours?

**LORENZO.** Yeah. Our mother's, and ours, too.

**MAXIMILIANO.** So where?

(OVERLEAF) **FIGURE 2.2** *The Whole of Time / El tiempo todo entero*, Espacio Callejón, Buenos Aires, September 2012. Actors (LEFT TO RIGHT): Esteban Bigliardi, Esteban Lamothe, and Pilar Gamboa. *Photograph by Sebastián Arpesella.*

**LORENZO.** Where what?

**MAXIMILIANO.** Your mom.

**LORENZO.** Out.

**MAXIMILIANO.** Oh, yeah, but she lives here.

**LORENZO.** Yeah, it's her place.

**MAXIMILIANO.** Oh, and that's your dad.

*Maximiliano's pointing to the painting. Antonia laughs.*

**LORENZO.** No, that's Frida Kahlo's father.

**MAXIMILIANO.** Oh.

**LORENZO.** It's a picture, a painting.

**MAXIMILIANO.** Yeah, I can tell it's a painting.

**LORENZO.** Yeah. What I'm saying is that we have it there like a painting, because it's a painting, a picture.

**MAXIMILIANO.** Yeah, I get it. A picture. Because you all like it or what?

**LORENZO.** My Mom brought it when we came back from Mexico.

**MAXIMILIANO.** You were in Mexico?

**LORENZO.** We're Mexican. We were born there.

**MAXIMILIANO.** What, your Mom's Mexican?

**LORENZO.** No, but she lived there for a while.

**MAXIMILIANO.** Uh-huh, and your old man?

*Maximiliano points at the painting again.*

**LORENZO.** No.

**ANTONIA.** Anyway, it's not that representative. That's why we like it. She usually painted portraits of herself.

**MAXIMILIANO.** He doesn't look Mexican.

**ANTONIA.** Because he isn't. He was Hungarian. Wilhelm. She loved him very much. He was a photographer.

**MAXIMILIANO.** She killed herself, right? The painter.

**ANTONIA.** Frida? No, not at all. She died from an accident she had when she was young. She spent her whole life dying.

**MAXIMILIANO.** I thought she was one of those who'd died by suicide.

**ANTONIA.** No! Well, even though her death is a little fuzzy, some say she took a cocktail of pills mixed with morphine, for the pain, because her body was split into a thousand pieces. But that's not the official version. She got tired of the pain.

**MAXIMILIANO.** Nope, don't know anything about her. Wasn't she kind of a hippie?

**ANTONIA.** Hippie? You mean because of her clothes? That's traditional Mexican clothing. It's really sophisticated, woven on a loom and hand-embroidered.

**MAXIMILIANO.** I didn't know, sorry. Why was her body split?

**ANTONIA.** She had an accident when she was young. She was on a trolleybus.

**MAXIMILIANO.** On a what?

**LORENZO.** They're like trams. It's just that my sister likes strange words.

**ANTONIA.** It's not strange, that's what it's called.

**LORENZO.** Are you interested in this story? It's a little gruesome.

**MAXIMILIANO.** Yeah, I'm interested.

**ANTONIA.** Well, she was on a tram . . .

**LORENZO.** Trolleybus, Antonia.

**ANTONIA.** And a car rammed into them and a handrail was driven into her groin.

**LORENZO.** She was impaled on it.

**ANTONIA.** It went right through her. She almost died. It was a miracle that she didn't. But her spine was gravely injured and she had to undergo infinite operations throughout her entire life. And she was in a cast and confined to bed for years at a time. Every so often she'd have a relapse.

**MAXIMILIANO.** Poor thing.

**ANTONIA.** Not poor thing, she was Frida Kahlo. She did all her painting in that condition. I think she had a beautiful life despite her physical suffering. She had a great sense of humor. Maybe that's what saved her.

**MAXIMILIANO.** Oh yeah?

**ANTONIA.** Yeah. On some of her paintings, actually a lot of them, she'd put titles or allusive or explanatory names, and the majority are very comical.

*Antonia goes over and points out to him the portrait of Frida Kahlo's father.*

**MAXIMILIANO** (*reading*): "I painted my father Wilhelm Kahlo" . . .

**ANTONIA.** Well, not that one.

*Antonia goes back to the computer. Lorenzo's reading, sitting on the corner bench.*

**MAXIMILIANO.** Do you like paintings, too?

**LORENZO.** Yeah, but not as much as my sister does.

**MAXIMILIANO.** We can go whenever you want.

**LORENZO.** Okay, relax. I only have twenty pages left. Do you mind?

**MAXIMILIANO.** No, no, go ahead and read.

(*Lorenzo gestures to offer Maximiliano a seat. Maximiliano sits down.*)

So what's it about?

**LORENZO.** There's a whaling ship that's going after a white killer whale.

**MAXIMILIANO.** An adventure story.

**LORENZO.** Yeah.

**MAXIMILIANO.** So how is it? Any good?

**LORENZO.** Yeah, it's good.

**MAXIMILIANO.** So what does she do?

**LORENZO.** Antonia?

**MAXIMILIANO.** Yes, what does she do, what's her job.

**LORENZO.** Ask her.

**MAXIMILIANO.** No, it's doesn't matter.

**LORENZO.** Antonia!

*Antonia turns around.*

**MAXIMILIANO.** No, I just asked your brother what you did.

**ANTONIA.** With what?

**MAXIMILIANO.** I don't know, with your life.

**ANTONIA.** You mean like a profession?

**MAXIMILIANO.** Yeah, I don't know, what do you do.

**ANTONIA.** Oh, nothing.

**MAXIMILIANO.** What do you mean nothing?

**ANTONIA.** Yeah, nothing. At least according to the terms you're asking me, nothing.

**MAXIMILIANO.** You don't work?

**ANTONIA.** No.

**MAXIMILIANO.** You study.

**ANTONIA.** Do you mean at the university?

**MAXIMILIANO.** Yes.

**ANTONIA.** Oh, no.

**MAXIMILIANO.** You must do something.

**ANTONIA.** No, I don't believe in doing.

**MAXIMILIANO.** In what way?

**ANTONIA.** In the way of doing. Doing for its own sake. Something, any-thing. I don't believe in that.

**MAXIMILIANO.** Like working?

**ANTONIA.** For example. I don't understand why they do those things. Working, going to school, traveling, going out.

**MAXIMILIANO.** But you must do something . . . You're over there at the computer. You talk; for example, you're talking with me now.

**ANTONIA.** Those are all strictly nonproductive things.

**MAXIMILIANO.** You think so?

**LORENZO.** Antonia doesn't go out.

**MAXIMILIANO.** You don't go out?

**LORENZO.** She doesn't like to leave her home.

**MAXIMILIANO.** She doesn't leave her home?

**LORENZO.** No.

**MAXIMILIANO.** She doesn't go outside?

**LORENZO.** No.

**MAXIMILIANO.** Like she doesn't go out on the sidewalk.

**LORENZO.** No.

**MAXIMILIANO.** Don't you want to go outside?

**ANTONIA.** I don't know, ask Lorenzo.

*Lorenzo is getting uncomfortable so he goes to another room to fin-ish his book. Maximiliano and Antonia are alone. After a while:*

**MAXIMILIANO.** Excuse me, can we listen to some music?

**ANTONIA.** Yes, we can.

**MAXIMILIANO.** Will it bother you if I put on a song?

**ANTONIA.** No.

**MAXIMILIANO.** But do you want to?

**ANTONIA.** It's all the same to me.

*Maximiliano hesitates, he doesn't understand.*

**MAXIMILIANO.** Would you rather we talked?

**ANTONIA.** Okay.

*Maximiliano is perplexed. He doesn't know what to say.*

**MAXIMILIANO.** Too bad you don't go out.

**ANTONIA.** Why?

**MAXIMILIANO.** Because you're pretty.

**ANTONIA.** How so?

**MAXIMILIANO.** I don't know, to me. I think you're pretty.

**ANTONIA.** Okay.

**MAXIMILIANO.** You're a person who could be normal, who could have a . . . normal life. I don't know, go out, meet people.

**ANTONIA.** Why.

**MAXIMILIANO.** To get to know them, talk. Have experiences.

**ANTONIA.** I don't know.

**MAXIMILIANO.** You're afraid.

**ANTONIA.** Afraid? I don't think so. I'm not interested.

**MAXIMILIANO.** How do you know?

**ANTONIA.** Because I used to go out on the street and then I quit going out.

**MAXIMILIANO.** Why?

**ANTONIA.** Because I didn't want to do it anymore. I just started staying here inside.

**MAXIMILIANO.** But they didn't send you to a psychologist or something.

**ANTONIA.** Who.

**MAXIMILIANO.** I don't know, your brother, your mom.

**ANTONIA.** No, they love me.

**MAXIMILIANO.** That's why.

**ANTONIA.** Like this, they love me the way I am. I'm like this.

**MAXIMILIANO.** Like how? You seem really smart to me.

**ANTONIA.** Okay.

**MAXIMILIANO.** Seriously, I'm sorry, I'm really sorry that nobody knows you.

**ANTONIA.** Why.

**MAXIMILIANO.** Because it's a waste, because you are a nice person. Smart and pretty.

**ANTONIA.** Waste? I don't like to go out. I don't like people in general. I like my brother and my mom.

**MAXIMILIANO.** You get along with your mom?

**ANTONIA.** No.

**MAXIMILIANO.** So? Is there anything I can do, for example, to make you want to go out?

**ANTONIA.** No.

**MAXIMILIANO.** Nothing, you already know that.

**ANTONIA.** It's that I don't want to go out. Don't ask me like that anymore, please. It bothers me. If you want, you can come here and we can talk, but about other things. Not about leaving or staying. This is who I am, I'm this way.

**MAXIMILIANO.** But don't you think it's sad?

**ANTONIA.** Sad? For who?

**MAXIMILIANO.** For you.

**ANTONIA.** I don't think so, I'm not sad. If you think this is sad, it's because you think something else is, I don't know, happy? What seems happy to you, what do you like to do?

MAXIMILIANO. Me?

ANTONIA. Uh-huh.

MAXIMILIANO. I don't know. I like talking to people, I like having free time.

ANTONIA. So.

MAXIMILIANO. What?

ANTONIA. You're saying I'm right, you like having free time. All of my time is what you'd call free.

MAXIMILIANO. Yeah. But no. I like having free time because it's free because the other time is busy.

ANTONIA. And if the other time isn't busy, like you say, what is it?

MAXIMILIANO. I don't know, wasted?

ANTONIA. Wasted. What is wasted time—the time when you're not working?

MAXIMILIANO. No, that's my free time.

ANTONIA. Oh, wasted time is mine then, for example.

MAXIMILIANO. I don't know. Maybe.

ANTONIA. So what would be not wasting it? Making money?

MAXIMILIANO. Even if it's not making money. Doing something, I don't know, even if it's something you like to do.

ANTONIA. I like to listen to music. Be at the computer. And read. And think. And be with my mom. And with my brother, too. And now with you. Afterwards I do some chores and I sleep. And I dream. That's what I do with my time.

MAXIMILIANO. Okay, fine.

*Pause.*

ANTONIA. Maxi . . .

MAXIMILIANO. What?

ANTONIA. What's your day like?

MAXIMILIANO. My day?

ANTONIA. Yeah, tell me about your day.

MAXIMILIANO. You mean, a typical day?

ANTONIA. A weekday, for example.

MAXIMILIANO. I don't do anything. I go to work and then I go home or I go out.

ANTONIA. No, no. Tell me all the details, everything you do.

MAXIMILIANO. Everything-everything?

ANTONIA. What time do you get up?

MAXIMILIANO. Oh, everything. Well, the alarm goes off at 8:30 and I turn over a couple of times and then it goes off again at 9 and then I get up.

ANTONIA. Every day?

MAXIMILIANO. Yeah, every day. Except for Mondays which I have off. Mondays or Tuesdays, they change them around on me.

ANTONIA. You get up at 9.

MAXIMILIANO. Yeah, I get up.

ANTONIA. What's the very first thing you do when you wake up?

MAXIMILIANO. Uh, well, usually I take a shower.

ANTONIA. But don't you do anything before that? You get out of bed and the first thing you do is jump in the shower?

MAXIMILIANO. Uh, no. The first thing I do is turn on the radio. I get up and click! I turn on the radio.

ANTONIA. AM or FM?

MAXIMILIANO. FM. I turn on the radio and I put on the water for my *mate*.[10] I go take a leak, wait for the water to get ready, drink a few

---

**10** *Mate* (pronounced *mah-tay*) is an herbal tea typical of the River Plate region. [Trans.]

sips of *mate* and then I get into the shower. I don't do much else. I drink my *mate*, check my email, I get dressed and around 10 I'm heading out the door.

ANTONIA. You don't eat anything?

MAXIMILIANO. No, I eat lunch at 11:30 at the grill. They feed us there.

ANTONIA. Of course. Go on, go on.

MAXIMILIANO. I work until around 5 and then it depends. Sometimes I go back home, other times I go for a walk or I meet up with someone. Thursdays I go play soccer and then eat with the guys from the grill . . . it depends.

ANTONIA. And if you go home after work?

MAXIMILIANO. I hardly ever go home right away.

ANTONIA. Okay, but if you do.

MAXIMILIANO. Well, if I do it's because I'm tired, so I take a nap or watch TV and afterwards I make something to eat or have it delivered.

ANTONIA. And out of those weeks, those days, which moment, which time would be what you called free before?

MAXIMILIANO. Hmm, let's see, when I leave work. From when I leave work until I have to go back. Even though I don't count mornings because I'm getting up and ready to go out. If I go to bed really late or drunk or something, I don't even make my *mate*, I just leave, and I go out into the street still half asleep.

ANTONIA. In other words, during your free time you like to be at home, watching television or sleeping, and that's what you enjoy, that's what you like to do.

MAXIMILIANO. Yeah, that too. Other times I go out, what I already told you.

ANTONIA. So, what do you find when you're out and walking around?

MAXIMILIANO. What do you mean what do I find?

ANTONIA. Yeah, during your free time, walking around the streets, what do you like about that.

MAXIMILIANO. Oh. Let's see. I don't know, spending a nice moment with somebody. Talking about something, drinking a beer, maybe hooking up. Walking around and seeing the city, the people. Sometimes things happen, strange things, or you happen to run into somebody by chance. Sometimes, not very often. But if you go out, that's a possibility. Or also getting to know someone new, I don't know.

ANTONIA. You meet a lot of people in the street.

MAXIMILIANO. Well, no.

ANTONIA. You met me here, for example. Here inside. And I met you here, too. I meet people here. And the people who come here usually are invited by my brother, my mom or me.

MAXIMILIANO. And what do they say?

ANTONIA. About what.

MAXIMILIANO. About you not going out.

ANTONIA. Nothing, they know. Are you really worried about my not going out, does it disturb you that much?

MAXIMILIANO. Do you want me to tell you the truth?

ANTONIA. Please.

MAXIMILIANO. I can't believe it.

ANTONIA. Why such a big deal?

MAXIMILIANO. I didn't even know that Lorenzo had a sister.

ANTONIA. What does that have to do with it, you must not have asked him. If I'd gone out, you probably wouldn't have known it either. That doesn't have anything to do with my not going out. I like to be here. Do you see this as a problem?

MAXIMILIANO. I believe it is a problem.

ANTONIA. According to whom?

MAXIMILIANO. I think a doctor would say so.

ANTONIA. A psychologist.

MAXIMILIANO. For example.

ANTONIA. It depends on what you're expecting, in reality.

MAXIMILIANO. In what way?

ANTONIA. You think I'm crazy for staying here inside. I seem crazy to you.

MAXIMILIANO. No, you don't seem crazy to me.

ANTONIA. So then?

MAXIMILIANO. But people who go to a psychologist aren't crazy. People, everybody, has some issue to resolve, something to get an answer for, something that's causing them distress and they go to the psychologist because it helps them to be better, I don't know.

ANTONIA. Do you go to a psychologist?

MAXIMILIANO. No.

ANTONIA. You never went?

MAXIMILIANO. No.

ANTONIA. So then?

MAXIMILIANO. Well, I don't know, I never had to, I never felt that bad.

ANTONIA. But I do? I feel bad?

MAXIMILIANO. I don't know. Do you feel bad?

ANTONIA. Sometimes, but like everyone. Not bad like resolving something or thinking that it's a problem.

MAXIMILIANO. Okay.

ANTONIA. Do I tell you that your life is weird and you ought to be another way and you seem weird to me because you go to work in the same place every day and you wait on people and you feed them only so you can feel just bad enough in order to feel good later, when you're off work? I don't need that kind of contrast in order to cope with time. I cope with all my time, the whole of my time, nonstop.

MAXIMILIANO. So what do you live on?

ANTONIA. The money my mom earns. And some of what my brother brings in.

MAXIMILIANO. And that doesn't make you feel bad?

ANTONIA. What?

MAXIMILIANO. Your brother works and you don't.

ANTONIA. No. My mom's is enough to live on. And my brother works because he wants to.

MAXIMILIANO. But he contributes.

ANTONIA. Because he wants to. I'm getting bored. I thought you were a little less normal. Sorry.

(*Maximiliano zips up his jacket in order to go. Antonia spontaneously goes over and kisses him. He lets her do it. He touches her hair; she becomes uncomfortable and moves away.*)

Does the concept of the bogeyman[11] mean anything to you?

MAXIMILIANO. Bogeyman? Like the little kids' bogeyman?

ANTONIA. The bogeyman, yeah, the scary one.

MAXIMILIANO. Yeah, what's up.

ANTONIA. Don't you feel him sometimes?

MAXIMILIANO. The bogeyman? Is that a saying?

ANTONIA. No, yeah, it's a hole here inside.

(*She points to her guts.*)

Don't you feel it?

---

**11** In the original, it is *cuco*, a ghost-monster. [Trans.]

**MAXIMILIANO.** I don't know, maybe I don't call it bogeyman. Are you talking about being afraid?

**ANTONIA.** It's fear. But it's also something else. Do you follow?

**MAXIMILIANO.** I don't know. But why are you telling me this.

**ANTONIA.** It doesn't matter.

**MAXIMILIANO.** Yeah, it interests me.

**ANTONIA.** It has to do with what we were talking about before.

**MAXIMILIANO.** Not going out?

*Antonia glares at him.*

**ANTONIA.** I love you.

*(Silence. Maximiliano stands up.)*

No. Just kidding, kidding.

*Antonia puts on Rata Blanca's "La leyenda del hada y el mago."*[12] *She goes over to Maximiliano and examines him closely: she studies his face, counts his moles, looks at his hands, smells them. He tries to kiss her, she stops him with a frozen embrace: she pins his arms with her own hug, he lets her, motionless. She goes behind him, pulls up his T-shirt and goes over his back, counting his moles. She then returns to face him, points to her own nape, he counts her moles, he takes her hair down, she doesn't like it but lets him do it, he messes up her hair, she suffers through it, she moves away, putting an end to the situation. Lorenzo comes back in, takes his book over to his sister and reads her the ending of* Moby-Dick.

*Maximiliano remains suspended in the middle of the room, ignored by the other two.*

**MAXIMILIANO.** Beautiful.

---

**12** Rata Blanca is an Argentina power metal band. The 1990 single's title is "The Legend of the Wizard and the Fairy." Originally sung in Spanish, the band later recorded a version in English. [Trans.]

*Ursula arrives.*

**URSULA.** Oh, thank God you're alive!

**LORENZO.** Awake, Mom. Thank God we're awake.

**URSULA.** Yes, thank God.

**LORENZO.** This is Maximiliano, from the grill.

**URSULA.** Hello, now I'll greet you properly, welcome, Lorenzo's friend. You a waiter, too?

**LORENZO.** He works at the bar.

**MAXIMILIANO.** I mix the drinks.

**URSULA.** Bartender! How wonderful, how much fun. Did you study for that, do you have a signature cocktail, something you're particularly good at, a favorite, something everybody orders?

**MAXIMILIANO.** My Bloody Marys are great.

**URSULA.** With tomato juice, yeah. I don't like drinks with a lot of pulp, they don't sit well with me, they seem heavy. If I want to get drunk, I don't feel like drinking a smoothie. Like that drink, what's the one that's popular these days, that you made for my birthday?

**ANTONIA.** Daiquiri.

**URSULA.** It's like a fruit smoothie with alcohol.

**LORENZO.** Daiquiri.

**URSULA.** Daiquiri, that's it. And anyway, the fruit ferments in the alcohol, and then what happens? You get drunk really fast, because it's sweet. Do you remember how we all ended up that day?

**LORENZO.** Some worse than others.

**URSULA.** Do you make daiquiris, Maximiliano? What an imperial name, Maximiliano.

**MAXIMILIANO.** It's a family name. My dad and my grandfather were named Maximiliano. Yeah, I do. Women ask for it a lot.

URSULA. Ask for what?

LORENZO. Daiquiris, Mom, what were we just talking about?

URSULA. I got a little dizzy. Bring your mother something strong, Lorenzo, bring me a digestif.

ANTONIA. I want one, too.

LORENZO. Maxi?

MAXIMILIANO. Sure.

URSULA. Maxi. Of course, because Maximiliano is really long. But it's nice, it's worth saying your whole name.

ANTONIA. I don't like drinks with fruit pulp.

URSULA. You like daiquiris . . . She drank a ton on my birthday.

ANTONIA. Because Lorenzo made them. And there wasn't anything else. But I wouldn't choose it as an alcoholic beverage.

URSULA. I like long names, Lorenzo, Antonia; and I like to say the whole name, I like that. Taking the time to name something, things.

ANTONIA. Your children, for example.

URSULA. Especially my children.

*Lorenzo comes back in with four small glasses and a bottle of some kind of herbal liqueur.*

MAXIMILIANO. Antonia and Lorenzo are nice, their names.

URSULA. Nice enough to say the whole names, because they aren't diminutiveable.

LORENZO. Diminutiveable.

URSULA. From diminutive, yes, they cannot be shortened. "Anton," "Loren"—it doesn't work.

ANTONIA. I like "Anton."

URSULA. It's awful, honey.

**ANTONIA.** I like it.

**URSULA.** And besides, "Anton" could be Antonella and Antonella is appalling.

*Lorenzo pours the drinks.*

**MAXIMILIANO.** It just so happens that my girlfriend's named Antonella.

**URSULA.** Seriously?

**MAXIMILIANO.** Yes, seriously . . .

(*An uncomfortable moment.*)

No, just kidding, kidding.

**URSULA.** Well, isn't he the fresh one, you're fresh you . . . So what if that were her name, what would be the problem, you had a girlfriend with an ugly name, that's that, why would we get worked up.

*They toast one another.*

**ANTONIA.** So, what is your girlfriend's name?

**MAXIMILIANO.** Mine? I don't have one.

**ANTONIA.** Come on, what's her name.

**MAXIMILIANO.** Sabrina.

**URSULA.** That's a nice name, too.

**MAXIMILIANO.** I don't like it.

**ANTONIA.** Because it's not that nice.

**LORENZO.** I didn't know you had a girlfriend.

**MAXIMILIANO.** Because I don't.

**LORENZO.** That little blond the other day? The one that was waiting for you on the corner outside the grill?

**MAXIMILIANO.** Yeah, yeah, but she's not my girlfriend!

(*An uncomfortable silence.*)

And what exactly is this made from?

**URSULA**. It is Pálinka, a Hungarian liqueur. It's made from roots and herbs. It's very healthy.

*Maximiliano tries it.*

**MAXIMILIANO**. And it has quite a bit of alcohol.

**ANTONIA**. This isn't Pálinka, Pálinka is made from fruit.

*The two siblings gulp it down and serve themselves some more.*

**MAXIMILIANO**. Hungary. Are you Hungarian?

**URSULA**. My family is. Ursula Cabjolski is my maiden name. My father came here in '23, on the . . .

**LORENZO**. *Caligaris.*

**URSULA**. You want to tell the story, Lorenzo?

**LORENZO**. No.

**URSULA**. Yes, on the *Great Caligaris*, when he was a boy, after the First World War, seeking his fortune. Theodor Cabjolsky.

**MAXIMILIANO**. Hungarian.

**URSULA**. Hungarian. Hard workers. They worked their hides off here. He had a pencil business, they imported stationery items. And then they started to make their own. And ink, they made ink for pens and stamps, back when they used ink.

**LORENZO**. As you can see, my mom's a little bit in love with her father.

**ANTONIA**. How did it go tonight, Uschi?

**URSULA**. How did it go with what?

**ANTONIA**. Your date, how did it go?

**URSULA**. What date, honey? I went out to eat.

**ANTONIA**. Okay, so how did it go?

**URSULA**. It went well, very well. We went to a really nice little place, specializing in fish. They're known for their freshwater fish. Everything was really delicious, really well prepared. And what about you? What did you do? Did you eat something? Were you chatting?

**LORENZO.** Here, just like you see us. Chatting a bit, listening to music, that kind of thing.

**URSULA.** Did you offer this boy something to eat?

**MAXIMILIANO.** Yes, but I don't want anything.

**URSULA.** But you offered.

**MAXIMILIANO.** Yes, yes, but I was already full.

**URSULA.** So what did you chat about?

**LORENZO.** Your family.

**URSULA.** My family? What about my family?

**LORENZO.** Their origins, the Hungarians.

**URSULA.** The Hungarians? And why did you talk about that?

**LORENZO.** Because of Maxi, the picture, because he asked and he wanted to know so I told him a bit, that's it.

*Maximiliano is uncomfortable.*

**URSULA.** Oh, yes? And where's your family from?

**MAXIMILIANO.** Italy. And Spain. Basque, on my mother's side.

**URSULA.** You look Basque. What's your last name?

**MAXIMILIANO.** Casas.

**URSULA.** Oh, no.

**MAXIMILIANO.** Yes, no, my mom's family from the Basque Country. But third generation.

**URSULA.** Of course. You know I've never been to the Basque Country, but it must be gorgeous.

**MAXIMILIANO.** No idea, they say so. It seems to be very green.

**URSULA.** Green, of course, it's the garden of Spain. And Euskera . . . Euskera.

**MAXIMILIANO.** What?

**URSULA.** Their language, Euskera, it's really distinctive . . .

**MAXIMILIANO.** Oh, yeah, yeah.

**URSULA.** Because it's a language whose roots aren't like any other language's, that's very strange, do you speak Basque?

**LORENZO.** How is he going to speak Basque, Mom?

**MAXIMILIANO.** No, the truth is no. A little bit of English and that's it.

**ANTONIA.** Why are you putting her on?

**LORENZO.** Who?

**ANTONIA.** Mom. They're making it all up, Mom, we didn't even talk about that, about your origins. We talked about why I don't go out, afterwards that one went off to read, he kissed me and afterwards we listened to music. Why are you making this stuff up? What, do you think you're funny?

**URSULA.** Okay, Antonia, that's no reason to get so worked up, they're joking around, where's your sense of humor.

**ANTONIA.** I was defending you, Mom.

**URSULA.** But I don't need any of you to defend me and even less when nobody's attacking me.

**ANTONIA.** Oh, then I don't understand anything.

**URSULA.** I only want to protect you, honey.

**ANTONIA.** You protect me?

**URSULA.** That's what I'm trying to do.

**ANTONIA.** That's how you protect me.

**URSULA.** As much as I can.

**ANTONIA.** Thanks, Ursula, you make me feel a lot better.

**URSULA.** My daughter has no skin.

**LORENZO.** Don't say that, Mom. She's not pathetic.

*Maximiliano tries to leave.*

**URSULA.** Your sister is too soft for this world or at least for this city.

**LORENZO.** Don't talk about her as if she wasn't here.

**URSULA.** I'm talking about her as if she were here, because in this house we don't have any secrets, here important things are discussed, debated.

**LORENZO.** Not when there are other people, Ursula, I'm begging you. This is pathetic.

**URSULA.** I have nothing to hide.

**ANTONIA.** That's what's sad.

**URSULA** (*to Antonia*). The only thing that consoles me is that you're going to have to put up with yourself for every second of your life.

**LORENZO.** Ursula, that's enough.

*His mother imitates him.*

**URSULA.** "Ursula, enough, Ursula, enough, Ursula enough." Enough who? Who's giving the orders around here? Are you "Lorenzo, the Just," "Lorenzo, the Justice Seeker"? Is Captain Old Navy now giving the orders in this house, ladies and gentlemen? Your time is up, "Lorenzo-Justice." Did you talk to your sister? Did he tell you?

*Lorenzo keeps holding his mother's gaze with increasing violence but giving her the chance to take it back, to say she's sorry.*

**LORENZO.** Tell her what, Mom?

**URSULA.** That you're leaving.

**LORENZO.** Where to?

**URSULA.** To go live in Spain, soon, alone, that you've got it all planned, that you have your little roll of Euros stuffed in your sock, that you're going to try your luck, the American dream. God knows what you're going to do . . .

*Lorenzo loses control and kisses his mother as if he were delivering*
*a blow. Afterward he goes over to his sister, but Antonia doesn't*
*move, she ignores him. She will not look at him again.*

**LORENZO.** Kid, Puni, that's not true about Spain, it's a lie. It's something I told Mom so she'd become more independent, so she'd get on with her own life, but I'm not leaving here, I don't want to leave here. I don't have enough money, not even enough for the trip and I wouldn't want to, I wouldn't even want to. That was something between her and me, something that I started to say to her so she'd become more independent, do you understand? So she'd get on with her life. But I don't want to go, I'm not going to go.

**ANTONIA.** Why not?

**LORENZO.** *You're* asking me that?

**ANTONIA.** We're not the same person. If I were you, I'd leave.

**MAXIMILIANO.** I'm leaving.

**LORENZO.** Already?

**MAXIMILIANO.** Well, yes.

**ANTONIA.** No, stay.

**MAXIMILIANO.** You think?

**URSULA.** Stay, Maximiliano.

**MAXIMILIANO.** Sure?

**ANTONIA.** Yes.

**LORENZO.** Pun . . .

**URSULA.** So I'll become more independent? Who are these people? What are they doing in my home?

**LORENZO.** Pun, I'm serious about what I said about Spain.

**ANTONIA.** I don't want to talk. And I don't want to listen either. Don't get mad.

(*Antonia gets up, leaves Lorenzo and goes over to Maximiliano.*)
Do you know who Marco Antonio Solís is?

**MAXIMILIANO.** I'm not sure, is that him?

*Antonia puts the song "No hay nada más difícil que vivir sin ti" back on. She takes Maximiliano over to the computer and shows him Marco Antonio Solís's concert video. Her brother stays suspended in the space. Antonia goes to sit with her mother on the bench. The two women cry, Lorenzo is devastated, Maximiliano watches the video. Antonia will never look at her brother again.*

*They listen to the song until it ends.*

THE END

**AUTHOR'S NOTE**

In the 1937 painting *Memory* (*The Heart*) [*Memoria* (*el Corazón*)], Frida portrays herself in a little leather jacket she started wearing when she was separated from Rivera, in defiance of his disapproval of European-style clothing.

The Frida in the painting wears this jacket, with a hole at the level of her chest. Where her heart should be there's a hole with a railing running through it. Through the hole in her chest, and behind, the sky and some clouds. The extracted organ lies on the sand, losing blood. Some of the blood goes into the earth, some runs to the sea. It decomposes alone, so very large.

Her heart, like that, now so far away, doesn't mean anything anymore.

FAUNA

*Fauna* premiered at Centro Cultural General San Martín in Buenos Aires in 2013. The play was directed by Romina Paula with assistant direction by Ramiro Bailiarini, set design by Alicia Leloutre and Matías Sendón, set construction by Ariel Baccaro, lighting design by Matías Sendón. The production manager was Sebastián Arpesella.

## CAST

| | |
|---|---|
| ACTRESS | Pilar Gamboa |
| DIRECTOR | Rafael Ferro |
| MARÍA LUISA | Susana Pampin |
| SANTOS | Esteban Bigliardi |

*Fauna*

TRANSLATED BY **April Sweeney** AND **Brenda Werth**

*"The camera is an instrument that teaches people how to see without a camera."*
—Dorothea Lange

*"Girls and boys, playing in the afternoon,*
*running through the gardens,*
*landscapes that sound like perfect melodies,*
*with verses by Rilke or Brooke,*
*the generous enthusiasm of young souls*
*capable of changing the world,*
*the beauty of sacrifice and ideals,*
*and love, and children, and friendship,*
*but the black void, the intermittent chill of the abyss?"*
—Juan L. Ortiz, "Sí, las rosas."[1]


## I. TODESERFAHRUNG / DEATH EXPERIENCE

**ACTRESS.** We know nothing of this leave-taking that
Is not shared with us. We have no reason
To show admiration and love or hate
To Death, so marvelously deformed

By the mouth of the tragic mask.
The world is still full of roles that we must play.

---

**1** Juan L. Ortiz, "Sí las rosas," *El alba sube* (1933–36) in *Obra completa* (Buenos Aires: Centro de Publicaciones Universidad Nacional del Litoral, 1996).

While we worry, whether or not we please,
So too will Death play, though not nicely.

But as you left, the stage cracked
To reveal a flash of the real, a fissure
Through which you departed: green of real green,
Real sunshine, real forest.

Playing we go on. Reciting lines learned
With blood and tears, now and then
Striking gestures; but your being, distanced
From us, separated from our play, can

Sometimes overwhelm us, like the consciousness
Of that reality sinking in,
So that for a while we are daring,
Acting life, not seeking applause.[2]

**DIRECTOR.** What was that?

**MARÍA LUISA.** That was Rilke, "Death Experience."

**DIRECTOR.** I'm not sure if it works for me; it seems too pretentious.

**MARÍA LUISA.** Pretentious? It's not at all pretentious. I think it's beautiful.

**DIRECTOR.** I'm not saying it's not nice; I'm just saying that it doesn't work for me.

**MARÍA LUISA.** Fauna read a lot of Rilke.

**DIRECTOR.** Yes, but that's not important. I mean, I'm not saying it's not important, but it's not relevant. That's what I'm saying. It sounds pretentious the way she did it right now, and besides that, the text doesn't really suit her.

---

**2** Romina Paula translates Rainer Maria Rilke's "Todeserfahrung" (1907). Our English translation takes into account both the original German and Paula's Spanish translation.

**MARÍA LUISA.** I think it's beautiful. And very believable.

**DIRECTOR.** Yes, but it's about theater, and everything becomes overly self-referential, too self-conscious.

**MARÍA LUISA.** Theater? Where exactly?

**ACTRESS.** "But as you left, the stage cracked . . . "

**DIRECTOR.** Yeah, right there.

**MARÍA LUISA.** But that's a metaphor. It's talking about death, "Death Experience." The stage referred to is the stage of life. It's a familiar trope, you know, that all the world's a stage. It's in Shakespeare and Calderón, it's an Elizabethan trope.

**DIRECTOR.** Okay, okay, thanks. I'm not saying it isn't, but what I'm saying is that I don't think it works for us, as interesting as it may be, but thank you anyway. I think it's better to stick to her story.

**MARÍA LUISA.** Fauna loved Rilke.

**DIRECTOR.** Yes, but, um . . . how should I put this, the truth doesn't necessarily matter, María Luisa.

**MARÍA LUISA.** But you said you came here to make a film about a life.

**DIRECTOR.** Yes, Luisa, but it's not a documentary. It's a work of fiction, based on the life of Fauna, but it's not a documentary about her life.

**MARÍA LUISA.** I think it's a beautiful poem.

**ACTRESS.** Okay, what if I were to try it again, maybe breaking it up a bit, I mean, to give it a more contemporary feel?

**DIRECTOR.** And what would that be like?

**ACTRESS.** Should we try it?

**DIRECTOR.** Yeah, sure, go for it.

**MARÍA LUISA.** Gallop away!

**ACTRESS.** What?

**MARÍA LUISA.** Gallop to the very end of the thought! What you just read was hard to understand, you didn't convey meaning through the *enjambment*. You see, the thought continues from one verse to the next. And she read it as though there were full stops in between. Because in the version that she has each line begins with a capital letter, and that doesn't take into account the *enjambment*. In the beginning, for example, when it says:

*We know nothing of this leave-taking that*
*is not shared with us. We have no reason*
*to show admiration and love or hate*
*to Death, so marvelously deformed*

*by the mouth of the tragic mask.*

There's *enjambment* there, do you see? And it goes on:

*The world is still full of roles that we must play.*
*While we worry, whether or not we please,*
*so too will death play, though not nicely.*

*But as you left, the stage cracked*
*to reveal a flash of the real, a fissure*
*through which you departed: green of real green,*
*real sunshine, real forest.*

*Playing we go on. Reciting lines learned*
*with blood and tears, now and then*
*striking gestures; but your being, distanced*
*from us, separated from our play, can*

*sometimes overwhelm us, like the consciousness*
*of that reality sinking in,*

*so that for a while we are daring,*
*acting life, not seeking applause.*

**ACTRESS.** I'm struck by the use of so many *ings*—this idea of action.

**MARÍA LUISA.** The gerunds. Yes, they give the poem a sense of the present, of action, of an occurrence, of something that's actually happening, of this theater that is life. It's my mother's translation.

**ACTRESS.** Really?

**MARÍA LUISA.** Didn't I tell you that she was mad for Rilke? But the gentleman here insists that it's not important.

**ACTRESS.** How lovely.

**DIRECTOR.** You're going to have to pay a little more attention if you want to be her.

**MARÍA LUISA.** You're much more beautiful, that may be to your advantage . . . Mother was enchanting, but not exactly what you'd call pretty.

**ACTRESS.** Well, thank you.

**MARÍA LUISA.** Oh no, don't thank me, actually I'm not sure it's a compliment . . . it might even be problematic for the film.

**DIRECTOR.** Or life.

**MARÍA LUISA.** Or life—, that I wouldn't know.

**DIRECTOR.** What do you mean? You're a very good-looking woman.

**MARÍA LUISA.** Good-looking? I don't know if I should thank you or tell you to fuck off.

**ACTRESS.** I think you're very pretty, Luisa.

**MARÍA LUISA.** You two don't think that you'll be able to win me over with flattery, do you? Because that's not going to happen.

*He that loves to be flattered is worthy o' the flatterer.*
*Heavens, that I were a lord!*

ACTRESS. Is that also Rilke?

MARÍA LUISA. No, that's Shakespeare, *Timon of Athens*. Have you read it? It's extremely funny:

> *To general filths*
> *convert o' the instant, green virginity!*
> *Do 't in your parents' eyes!*
> *Son of sixteen,*
> *pluck the lined crutch from thy old limping sire,*
> *with it beat out his brains!*

> *Lust and liberty*
> *creep in the minds and marrows of our youth,*
> *that 'gainst the stream of virtue they may strive*
> *and drown themselves in riot!*[3]

DIRECTOR. Is that Shakespeare?

MARÍA LUISA. Yes, isn't it hilarious?

ACTRESS. Did she read Shakespeare as well?

MARÍA LUISA. She read everything that she could get her hands on. And she read German, English, French. Once she even tried learning Russian so that she could read the classics, but to be honest I'm not sure if she ever succeeded.

DIRECTOR. So, where are all of those books?

MARÍA LUISA. Oh no, they weren't her books. She didn't have enough money to buy books. She got them from the university library or borrowed them from her colleagues in the Poets' Circle. She herself probably only owned around ten books at the most.

---

3 William Shakespeare, *Timon of Athens* (1462), in *The Riverside Shakespeare* (G. Blakemore Evans ed.) (Boston, MA: Houghton Mifflin, 1974), 4.1.6–8, 14–15, 25–28.

DIRECTOR. Ah, so that's yet another bit of misinformation—the room stacked to the ceiling with books, books in different languages, first editions, incunabula.

MARÍA LUISA. That might be true for someone else but not for Fauna and not in this house! But if you want, we can ask the university library if they have any record of that time.

DIRECTOR. Sure, we can do that, but in my mind I already had the image of the room's walls lined from floor to ceiling with books. In my mind that treasure existed.

ACTRESS. Why did you say "another bit of misinformation"? What other inconsistencies have you come across?

DIRECTOR. The thing about the three marriages. It's completely untrue. She was only married once.

MARÍA LUISA. There was no way she was going to get married again. No way in hell; and the first time she got married was only because she was a minor and wanted to get out of the house. Otherwise she never would have gotten married at all.

DIRECTOR. And otherwise you wouldn't even exist, María Luisa. So don't laugh too hard.

MARÍA LUISA. Oh I'm laughing all right. I'm definitely laughing. It's impossible not to—if I can't laugh what else is there?

ACTRESS. What? And she got divorced later on?

MARÍA LUISA. No, there was no need to. They were good friends with Ramón, my father. He was also an extraordinary man, just marvelous. They loved each other very much.

ACTRESS. Hmm.

DIRECTOR. He was a poet, too. Together they would go to the university, where she audited classes and attended the Poets' Circle meetings.

**ACTRESS.** And that's how she dressed to go to the meetings and to school?

**MARÍA LUISA.** As a man, yes, she went as a man because otherwise they wouldn't let her in.

**ACTRESS.** To the university?

**DIRECTOR.** Women were prohibited from attending the university.

**ACTRESS.** Yes, I know, but I thought that was much earlier.

**MARÍA LUISA.** No, it wasn't, actually.

**ACTRESS.** And who's going to play Ramón? Or will there be no Ramón?

**DIRECTOR.** The truth is I really don't know yet, but one possibility is that Santos could play him. We were going to do some rehearsals with him if he's interested.

**MARÍA LUISA.** Yes, I already mentioned it and he wants to do it. He was very excited about it.

**ACTRESS.** Is Santos your husband?

**MARÍA LUISA.** Never in my wildest dreams would it occur to me to put the two words Santos and husband together.

**DIRECTOR.** He's the brother.

**MARÍA LUISA.** He's my brother, yes, and he's very particular.

**ACTRESS.** You've already met him?

**DIRECTOR.** No, not yet, he's out and about, in the woods.

**MARÍA LUISA.** Not in the woods, exactly. To be more precise, he's on the river. But he should be coming back soon. It's been a couple of days since he left.

**ACTRESS.** What does he do on the river?

**MARÍA LUISA.** He rows up the delta with Monito. They fish and sleep under the open sky. Santos is a bit feral. He grew up exposed to the elements. Let's just say that walls don't suit him. "He shows inclinations of a sultan, he's reminiscent of a savage, and he airs the pretensions of a priest." That's the way my mother described him.

DIRECTOR. And he has a monkey?

MARÍA LUISA (*laughing*). No! For being artists, you're all so literal, hmm? Monito is a boy, his friend, his pet.

ACTRESS. His pet?

MARÍA LUISA. That's what I call him because he treats him like a pet, but he lets him, you know. They're joined at the hip.

ACTRESS. But will he want to work on a film if he's so wild?

MARÍA LUISA. When he sees you he won't be able to refuse.

ACTRESS. This woman is something else.

DIRECTOR. Didn't I tell you?

ACTRESS. And she's not going to be in the film? Couldn't she play an older Fauna?

DIRECTOR. Possibly.

MARÍA LUISA. No, no way, you won't be putting me in front of a camera.

DIRECTOR. I think it might be better if she advises you.

MARÍA LUISA. Yes, definitely.

ACTRESS. I'm wondering about Santos. And if he doesn't want to or can't do it, maybe you could do it. Play Ramón, I mean.

MARÍA LUISA. Are you an actor, too?

DIRECTOR. No, and I have no intention of playing the part of Ramón. That's her idea.

ACTRESS. I think he could be a great actor, he's very histrionic, you'll see once you get to know him.

MARÍA LUISA. Are you two sleeping together . . . ? I hope the question doesn't offend you but you seem like a couple.

**DIRECTOR.** Appearances can be deceiving, María Luisa, you should know that better than anyone.

**MARÍA LUISA.** Why?

**DIRECTOR.** With all of your quoting, don't you have one for this particular situation? One about appearances that are deceiving?

**MARÍA LUISA.** Why of course:

> *Woe to thee, in thy pride so powerful seeming, without knowing*
> *thou art dreaming!*
> *Yet be warned and on thee take: ways more mild and beseeming, for*
> *but perhaps thou art but dreaming, when it seems that thou 'rt*
> *awake.*[4]

**DIRECTOR.** Are you talking to me?

**MARÍA LUISA.** It's Calderón's *Life Is a Dream.*

**ACTRESS.** Okay, I'll be right back.

*She leaves.*

**MARÍA LUISA.** You seem like a couple. There's nothing wrong with that.

**DIRECTOR.** But we're not. We work together. And anyway, you started by asking if we were sleeping together.

**MARÍA LUISA.** Aren't you?

**DIRECTOR.** Is it that important to you? Do you need to know that for some reason?

**MARÍA LUISA.** No, but it might be helpful, for the film, if you have to play Ramón's part.

**DIRECTOR.** I highly doubt it. And anyway, I'm married and have two kids.

**MARÍA LUISA.** Congratulations.

---

**4** Pedro Calderón de la Barca, *Life Is a Dream* (Denis Florence Mac-Carthy trans.) (London: Henry S. King, 1873), 1317–19 (2.3); 1528–31 (2.6).

**DIRECTOR.** Thank you.

**MARÍA LUISA.** You're in love.

**DIRECTOR.** Oh, is that so? With whom?

**MARÍA LUISA.** With Julia.

**DIRECTOR.** Just artistically.

**MARÍA LUISA.** Really?

**DIRECTOR.** Yes, really.

**MARÍA LUISA.** Like a muse.

**DIRECTOR.** Something like that.

**MARÍA LUISA.** She's very beautiful.

**DIRECTOR.** Yes.

**MARÍA LUISA.** You're also very well put together, eh?

**DIRECTOR.** Is that so? Well put together? Are you getting back at me for "good-looking"?

**MARÍA LUISA.** No, I had already forgotten about that. I can call you sexy if you'd like.

**DIRECTOR.** No, I'll stick with well put together.

**MARÍA LUISA.** I think that Santos will be useful to you. He's a little like you, like an undomesticated version of you.

**DIRECTOR.** Oh really?

**MARÍA LUISA.** Yes, untamed.

**DIRECTOR.** And what did you think of the girl, Luisa? Do you think she can play the part of Fauna?

**MARÍA JULIA:** Julia? I think so . . . You say she's a good actress.

**DIRECTOR.** Yes, but I'm not asking you that. I'm asking you about the feeling you get from her, when you think of your mother, of the figure of Fauna.

MARÍA LUISA. Oh . . . I think so . . . there is a resemblance, although she's prettier. I already told you that . . . But that's what film tries to do, right? To glamorize?

DIRECTOR. No, not always. It aestheticizes, yes, but in what sense do you mean?

MARÍA LUISA. No, I think I was just provoking you, don't pay any attention to me, Director.

DIRECTOR. You can be less formal with me, Luisa.

MARÍA LUISA. No, I don't feel that's necessary, thank you. But yes, I do feel that girl Julia possesses strength, an inner life, and I think that's the most important thing, right? When I think about my mother, well, you saw pictures of her. Did you see those eyes? They never lost their brilliance, you know? They were always like that until her dying day.

DIRECTOR. Have you always lived here?

MARÍA LUISA. Yes, I was born in this house, Mother gave birth to me here, upstairs, squatting down, she shat me out and into the world I came. That was common in these parts, it's how it was done and it seemed like a good idea to my mother. She had Santos that way too. I saw it all, I was standing next to her. I saw his birth, literally. So we've always lived with her, yes.

DIRECTOR. And you didn't have any other siblings? It was just the two of you?

MARÍA LUISA. And Athos, who was stillborn. He was Santos's twin. No, that's not quite right. He wasn't born dead. Actually he was born and died right there. I witnessed his birth and death, one thing right after the other: he came out, took a breath, released one loud cry, and stopped breathing. Fauna and I patted him and bathed him, Mother tried to breathe for him, but there was nothing we could do. So it's just the two of us.

FIGURE 3.1 *Fauna*, Espacio Callejón, Buenos Aires, 2013. Actors (LEFT TO RIGHT): Pilar Gamboa and Susana Pampín. *Photograph by Sebastián Arpesella.*

**DIRECTOR.** And Monito?

**MARÍA LUISA.** What about Monito? Monito is a boy from the river. Now, Monito is wild. You won't have the chance to see him. He's pretty skittish.

**DIRECTOR.** And do you have kids?

**MARÍA LUISA.** No, no. Not me. I kept my mother company until the very end. One day she couldn't get on her horse and the next day she died. She lay down to take a nap and never woke up.

**DIRECTOR.** Ninety-nine years.

**MARÍA LUISA.** Eight. They say ninety-nine because the double nine sounds nice, and because it makes her sound older. There will never be anyone like her.

*Julia enters dressed like a man.*

**ACTRESS.** Thank you, Luisa, for your hospitality. You have a beautiful home.

**MARÍA LUISA.** Did you find everything to your liking?

**ACTRESS.** Yes, thank you. But while I was unpacking I realized that I brought the wrong clothes. It didn't occur to me to pack for anything other than cool weather.

**DIRECTOR.** Why did you put those clothes on?

**ACTRESS.** I prefer to wear this while we're here, to acclimate myself. Do you mind, Luisa?

**MARÍA LUISA.** No, on the contrary. Anything you need, just let me know. I have lots of Fauna's clothing. This is hers, as a matter of fact. Now, what I don't understand is why you didn't bring a camera if you're going to make a film.

**DIRECTOR.** Well, because we're not quite there yet, at least not quite ready to begin filming. We came to do some research first and to meet you. All of you.

**MARÍA LUISA.** And Julia, too? Is it necessary for the actress to be here at this point?

**ACTRESS.** I wanted to come.

**DIRECTOR.** She's been involved in the project from the beginning. Actually, she's the one who told me about Fauna in the first place.

**MARÍA LUISA.** Oh, is that so? Did you meet her?

**ACTRESS.** I did, indeed. Didn't I tell you?

**DIRECTOR.** No.

**ACTRESS.** Ah, well, actually that's why we're here. I was here a couple of years ago. There was this torrential rainfall . . .

**MARÍA LUISA.** The flood.

**ACTRESS.** Yes, and I got stranded here. And one day I saw her passing by. It was like an apparition. I was standing under the eaves of the house where I was staying and suddenly out of the vibrant-green, rain-drenched grove, there emerged a woman on horseback, well, a person, I wasn't sure what I was seeing at first, and suddenly there appeared this powerful horse.

**MARÍA LUISA.** Zaino.

**ACTRESS.** And on this horse, there was something like an effigy, this being, this powerful person wearing a large hat: a stunning, magnificent, inscrutable, being covered by oversized plastic bags for protection against the rain. A face peered out between the folds of black and those brilliant eyes looked into mine for a brief second. I can't explain what I felt—it was like I was in shock. I wasn't sure if the terror I felt had to do with the possibility of danger, but at the same time it wasn't only terror, it was something more, something closer to pleasure, even idolatry? It lasted a second, then the reins shortened, the horse neighed and the apparition galloped away down the dirt path.

**MARÍA LUISA.** That was Zaino. And that was my mother.

**ACTRESS.** Afterwards, I asked around, and what do you know, the stories started coming out of the woodwork. Everyone had something to say about her and I was fascinated. I wanted to meet her, but they recommended against it. They said she was shy and lived her life surrounded by lunatics. . .

**MARÍA LUISA.** Lunatics? They couldn't have meant us! (*She erupts into terrifying laughter.*)

**ACTRESS.** So a couple of days went by and finally I was able to leave, but I couldn't get the image of this being out of my mind. Later I met up with José Luis to tell him about the trip and your mother.

He was looking for material for a film, and that's why he came here the first time and contacted you.

MARÍA LUISA. But in the meantime my mother had the audacity to die.

ACTRESS. Exactly.

MARÍA LUISA. So you must have seen her one of the last times she rode her horse.

ACTRESS. That's crazy.

MARÍA LUISA. And you say that she looked at you.

ACTRESS. Well, I'm not completely sure. It felt like she did, but maybe she wasn't actually looking at me.

MARÍA LUISA. She had perfect eyesight.

ACTRESS. I'm not sure, truthfully.

DIRECTOR. And her horse?

MARÍA LUISA. I don't know. He ran away or went somewhere to die. My mother died and we never saw the horse again. He could have died from sadness, I suppose . . .

(*She pricks up her ears to listen. The others watch her expectantly.*)

Santos.

*She leaves.*

ACTRESS. My God, there's so much information.

DIRECTOR. How are you? Did you have a good trip?

ACTRESS. Yeah, I'm good. It was long but good.

DIRECTOR. I really wanted to see you.

ACTRESS. What did you tell her?

DIRECTOR. Luisa?

ACTRESS. Yeah, did you tell her about us?

DIRECTOR. Are you crazy?

ACTRESS. So how did she know?

DIRECTOR. I don't know. She must have figured it out.

ACTRESS. What?

DIRECTOR. Julia . . .

ACTRESS. I wanted to talk to you about it anyway.

DIRECTOR. What?

ACTRESS. I prefer that we keep our distance here.

DIRECTOR. What do you mean by distance?

ACTRESS. I mean distance. I mean, I think we should be work colleagues and that's it.

DIRECTOR. But why?

ACTRESS. I don't know. It's not good for me to mix everything. I prefer to concentrate on the film, on Fauna.

DIRECTOR. Yes, of course, but what does that have to do with anything? I couldn't wait for you to get here and to have you to myself for a while.

ACTRESS. That's what I mean. I won't be able to be all yours right now, not even for a minute. I need to concentrate on the work and getting to know these people, who from what I've seen are interesting and very much worth our time.

DIRECTOR. Well, I don't know what to say. Am I allowed to even kiss you?

ACTRESS. No.

DIRECTOR. Why? I don't understand.

ACTRESS. I don't want to talk about this anymore. I'd prefer to have a working relationship, or a romance that evolves through our work, and of course we can still be friends. But if that's not possible, it's also not necessary.

DIRECTOR. It's not clear to me when you started thinking this way, Julia.

ACTRESS. I've been thinking about it for a long time. On the bus ride here everything came together and I knew I wanted to talk to you about it.

DIRECTOR. I can't believe this is happening to me.

ACTRESS. We came here to work.

DIRECTOR. What does that have to do with anything?

ACTRESS. It has everything to do with everything. I don't want to think about anything else. I want to concentrate on this person, on her life, and nothing else. I don't want to have to wonder what it means if we're sleeping together or not, or if you're looking at me this way or that. I just don't want to anymore.

DIRECTOR. Well, that's fine with me. The film is the most important thing for me, too.

ACTRESS. Fantastic.

DIRECTOR. Yes, fantastic.

*Silence*

ACTRESS. That woman is one of a kind.

DIRECTOR. But a little intrusive, don't you think?

ACTRESS. Intrusive? No, she didn't seem that way to me at all. Actually, she seems intelligent, charismatic, charming.

DIRECTOR. Well, you just met her.

ACTRESS. What does that have to do with anything? Plus, there's something about her that's profoundly familiar to me, as if I've known her forever.

DIRECTOR. As in another life?

ACTRESS. Maybe. And anyway it's not worth it for you to get upset about what I said. When the trip is over we can talk about it again if you want.

DIRECTOR. We'll see.

ACTRESS. What does "we'll see" mean?

## II. A LOVE SO BEAUTIFUL

*Santos arrives with reins in his hands, carrying an air of Horacio Quiroga.*

SANTOS. The artists!

(*For a few minutes they observe each other: Santos, Julia and José Luis. They all look at one another.*)

I have something for you artists that is real, something true . . . Have you ever staged a death? Or even witnessed one? Or is it not necessary in order to imagine it? No, of course not . . . I'm going to tell you about the death of something big, something majestic. It's hot and Monito and I go down to the river to bathe. We leave Lighting and Amber in the green pasture, in the shade, and in the sweltering heat we jump into the river to cool off. We let the current drag us along as we swim downstream and before we hit the sandbar we return to the riverbank and the shade, each of us too exhausted to walk. Monito sleeps, I sleep. Later that night, Monito awakens and I follow. We walk back upstream. It's already dark, the green foliage is thick, and it's not easy to find our way back or the animals we're looking for. Monito hollers for Amber and I for Lightning. There's nothing until a noise draws us near, a loud buzzing, a steady droning. They're bees, says Monito, and they are. We want to leave, back away, but then Monito gets closer. He hears the intense buzzing of a swarm of bees. He sees the bees attacking the horses and devouring them. No longer standing, they now lie motionless, mares with still hearts, they walk no more, they want no more. The two bodies are even darker at night, engulfed by bees that have left nothing—not even a hair or piece of flesh. Monito jumps into the swarm flailing his arms wildly and sends the bees flying, making it so dark that I can't see. Then I wave a piece of clothing and the bees take flight, sounding like an engine as they rise up together. And while we untangle the mares from the reins that held them captive, the bees attack us and we run back to the water and swim away. Only water will stop them. So there we are, in the cold of the night, swimming to escape the bees and save ourselves from being eaten alive. Because they won't stop . . . And in the water Monito seems to weep, for the mares, the sweet mares: large, black and lying together side by side, unmoving, and nothing can be done.

ACTRESS. *But as you left, the stage cracked*
*to reveal a flash of the real, a fissure*
*through which you departed: green of real green,*
*real sunshine, real forest.*

It's Rilke, translated by your mother.

SANTOS. Yes. And you, what would you do? How would you do it? With such a large horse lying motionless on the ground?

DIRECTOR. How tragic.

SANTOS. But how would you do it?

DIRECTOR. Do what?

SANTOS. Represent it.

DIRECTOR. The death?

SANTOS. The horses.

DIRECTOR. Ah, no, I don't know.

SANTOS. You don't know?

DIRECTOR. No.

SANTOS. You don't know.

**DIRECTOR.** No. I don't know anything about horses. Well, very little.

**SANTOS.** Do you want to go see?

**DIRECTOR.** The horses?

**SANTOS.** Yeah.

**DIRECTOR.** No.

**ACTRESS.** I would go.

**DIRECTOR.** To see the horses? What for?

**SANTOS.** You have to help me bury them.

**DIRECTOR.** The horses? They have to be buried?

**SANTOS.** I can't do it alone and Monito isn't coming back. He ran off. We won't see him for a few days. We have to dig.

**DIRECTOR.** Forgive me, but no. With all due respect, Santos, because, like I said, I haven't the slightest idea, but is it really necessary to bury them? What I mean is, aren't they already a part of nature? What I'm getting at is, isn't burying them more like a city thing?

**SANTOS.** If we don't bury them, the weasels will eat them bit by bit and burrow inside.

*Julia and José Luis look nauseated.*

**DIRECTOR.** Okay, no, yes, right, I have no problem with that . . . And we have to bury both of them, right? (*Julia gives him a disapproving look.*) Whenever you want, we'll do it.

**SANTOS.** Now.

**DIRECTOR.** Like at this very moment, now?

**SANTOS.** Night is the witching hour of the weasel.

*They leave.*

**MARÍA LUISA.** I'll tell you the whole story down to the very last detail. That way you'll be able to play the part well. I already told José Luis because he asked me about it so he could write the scene. It's like this: way before she became Fauna, when she was just a little girl from the province, my mother fell in love with a man.

**ACTRESS.** Your father.

**MARÍA LUISA.** No! Oh god no. She met my father later on. No, this was her first and only love, the one that destroyed her heart and mind forever. This man, who shall remain nameless, was much older than her; actually, he was a friend of her father's. She fell madly in love with him. She must have been fourteen or fifteen years old.

**ACTRESS.** Oh, so young.

**MARÍA LUISA.** How old are you?

**ACTRESS.** Older. And I'm still nowhere near getting married.

**MARÍA LUISA.** Good for you. So anyway, as a little girl my mother falls in love. This man, he marries her, whisks her away, and they spend a few happy months together. Or that's what they say. But apparently the old man was rather cunning, a very seductive womanizer. So, once the girl, his little trophy, is installed in his home, he returns to his carousing ways. At first, Fauna doesn't realize what's going on, because she's so enamored of him. She admires him deeply and is happy to have a house of her own where she can spend the whole day reading in the shade of a tree and taking long walks. She has a maid who does everything for her, a mix of mother, friend, and servant, so she doesn't have to worry about a thing. Her husband-father also spoils her and lets her do what she wants. But, as with all good things in life, this idle happiness is as fleeting as a sigh. One day he comes home and tells her that he has fallen in love with another woman and that he's going to leave her. He tells her he'll leave the house and the maid to her and that she will never want for anything but that he can't stay. He's fallen in love with another woman and is going to leave her so he can get married.

ACTRESS. How awful! And Fauna?

MARÍA LUISA. Little Fauna is left speechless. The man packs up his bags and says goodbye to her with a kiss on the forehead. My mother is in a state of shock for a couple of days but carries on with her life as usual. She eats, bathes, reads, takes walks. The only thing she doesn't do is talk. The maid tries a couple of times but to no avail. It's as if she'd exiled herself from her own body. One morning the maid wakes up and Fauna isn't there. Her things are there, her bed is unmade, as if she'd slept in it. The only thing that's missing is a bundle of clothes, nothing else. A few days go by and no sign of Fauna. Nobody knows anything, nobody's seen her; it's as if she'd evaporated into thin air. In desperation, the maid contacts the man to tell him what happened. He's concerned and begins to look for her everywhere. He feels guilty and doesn't want his conscience burdened by any misfortune. Then, one day, they contact him from Salta, and they tell him that in a small hotel in Cachi there's a young woman whose appearance matches the description of Fauna Forteza, the woman they've been looking for, who's been staying there for several weeks. But her name isn't Fauna Forteza. The man travels to Cachi and goes to the hotel. In the hotel lounge he sees Fauna, dressed like a lady, playing rummy with the hotel guests. She's laughing and having fun, and she's acquired the gestures and airs of a woman. Between laughs, Fauna raises her eyes from the game and sees him, but doesn't look at him. That is, she registers him visually but she doesn't react to his presence. It's as if she'd never seen him before in her life. The man calls her by her name but nobody at the table seems to care. He tries again, this time a little louder, and then everyone looks at him, but only because his attempt is so brash. One of the players asks him if he's looking for someone. Yes, he says, a guest, and they send him to reception, where he inquires about the pretty woman playing cards at the table. His blood runs cold when they tell him that the woman in question is none other than Martina Céspedes.

ACTRESS. And who is Martina Céspedes?

MARÍA LUISA. My mother had checked in under the name of the woman her husband left her for.

ACTRESS. No! How awful. And then what?

MARÍA LUISA. The man is profoundly shaken, he realizes that he is the cause of my mother's emotional upheaval and he doesn't leave her side until she recovers. Although she never fully recovers, really.

ACTRESS. So, he left her again?

MARÍA LUISA. No, as soon as she was doing better and had partially recovered her memory, she's the one who left. And it was in the Poets' Circle where she met my father. And that's where the story that you know a little bit about begins, the story of Fauno, who was once Fauna.

ACTRESS. But wait a second, so did she have amnesia? Or was she just pretending not to recognize him?

MARÍA LUISA. I don't know. No one knows for sure one way or the other. In principle it seems likely that she became disoriented and disassociated herself, and that at one point she really thought she was Martina Céspedes. Or maybe it was the only name she remembered.

ACTRESS. It's an incredibly sad story.

MARÍA LUISA. Yes, it's one of the most turbulent times of my mother's life. She never wanted to talk about it.

ACTRESS. And how did you find out?

MARÍA LUISA. Because of her notebooks from when she was being treated for amnesia and was trying to recover her memory. A part of the process involved writing down the little that she remembered and what others told her about herself. She wrote down everything in order to recover her identity. Those notebooks contain the whole story, well, not all of it, because there are still a lot of loose ends and there are a lot of unknowns, but it's more or less all there. And that's the scene the director wanted to write, the reunion scene, where the man finds Fauna and approaches her to ask her why she fled and whether or not she took that name as a form of revenge.

ACTRESS. José Luis is crazy.

## IV. FAUNA / FIRST REHEARSAL

*Santos and Julia are rehearsing the amnesia-reunion scene. María Luisa and José Luis watch.*

ACTRESS. I don't mean to be rude, but I'm telling you in all seriousness that I know nothing of what you say.

SANTOS. Fauna, it's me.

ACTRESS. You seem like a good man, but please don't insist. I don't know who Fauna is. My name is Martina Céspedes and you, sir, you I have never seen in my life.

SANTOS. I don't understand why you insist on torturing me like this, Fauna. I've already asked for your forgiveness.

ACTRESS. Sir, if you don't leave I am going to have to ask the maître d' to escort you out with force.

**SANTOS.** Fauna, please, forgive me. Do it for the love you once felt for me.

**ACTRESS.** Oh please, don't be ridiculous—what is this love you're talking about? Ha. Love. How presumptuous.

**SANTOS.** Fauna, it's me. What's happened to you? What have they done to you?

**ACTRESS.** Sir, please, I'm begging you.

**DIRECTOR.** Cut, cut . . . Very good Santos, it's good, thank you . . . Julia, listen to me, here you have to raise the stakes. If not, it turns into a sort of endless cycle that never builds. Do you understand? The guy is desperate because he doesn't know if she's lying or not.

**MARÍA LUISA.** Right, in fact, that was something that was never proven.

**DIRECTOR.** Exactly. So what you have to do is to play that—that ambiguity. Do you understand? Make us doubt whether or not you really had a bout of amnesia or if you just want revenge. I'm not saying it's easy, hmm? I imagine it's something like . . . (*José Luis gets ready to play the scene with Santos; however, this makes Santos a bit uncomfortable.*) What is it that you say here? Give me the line. (*Santos doesn't react.*) Give me a line from the text.

**SANTOS.** Which one?

**MARÍA LUISA.** How about taking it from "Do it for the love you once felt for me."

**DIRECTOR.** Yes, let's see, let's take it from there. Give me the line.

**SANTOS.** Fauna, please, forgive me. Do it for the love you once felt for me.

**DIRECTOR.** Oh please, don't be ridiculous—what is this love you're talking about? Ha. Love. How presumptuous.

**SANTOS.** Fauna, it's me. What's happened to you? What have they done to you?

**DIRECTOR.** Sir, please, I'm begging you.

**SANTOS.** If you insist on refusing me I am going to have to kidnap you.

**DIRECTOR.** So here is where something clicks. We should be able to see that she understands or remembers something, even if it's just the slightest glimmer.

**ACTRESS.** Ah, but we hadn't gotten to that part yet. You cut me off before that.

**DIRECTOR.** Really? Well, all the same you were missing the build. Let's try it again.

**MARÍA LUISA.** The director's not half bad, huh? Why don't you do the whole thing again without stopping and that way Santos can watch and learn.

**ACTRESS.** I'm sorry, can I say something? I like this scene, it seems powerful to me in its own right, but what I don't understand— and I'm thinking about the film here—is why we've chosen such a peculiar moment in Fauna's life to start with? A moment that's clearly sad and traumatic and shows her to be weak and con- fused . . . I'm sorry José, I'm not trying to undermine you, but wouldn't it be better to start from the moment she begins to dress as a man and joins the Poets' Circle? The moment she transforms into Fauno?

**MARÍA LUISA.** Hmm, there's an idea.

**ACTRESS.** Because it seems to me that the story is beautiful and full of pathos and I'm grateful to Luisa for sharing it and it's useful for all of us to know, but I wouldn't use it to create Fauno's character. It doesn't seem just.

(OVERLEAF) **FIGURE 3.2** *Fauna*, Espacio Callejón, Buenos Aires, 2013. Actors (LEFT TO RIGHT): Rafael Ferro, Esteban Bigliardi, Pilar Gamboa, and Susana Pampín. *Photograph by Sebastián Arpesella.*

**DIRECTOR.** That may well be, but that's beside the point. The episode reveals her to be vulnerable, not weak. That's what I like most about the scene.

**ACTRESS.** But she was only fifteen years old, José Luis.

**DIRECTOR.** Exactly, it's a foundational anecdote.

**ACTRESS.** That she never wanted to tell again, right—María Luisa? We have to respect that. Besides, it's not as if we're lacking anecdotes to choose from Fauno's life; we could make a six-hour film if we wanted to.

**SANTOS.** It's a story Mother wrote.

**MARÍA LUISA.** What is?

**SANTOS.** The one about amnesia. It's just a story—she told it to me as a story.

**MARÍA LUISA.** But it's in her recovery notebooks.

**SANTOS.** Did you read those notebooks?

**MARÍA LUISA.** No, but they exist.

**SANTOS.** Says who?

**MARÍA LUISA.** Mother.

**SANTOS.** I'm telling you, that story's a lie.

**DIRECTOR.** It's okay either way. Sorry, I don't mean to interrupt, but for the purposes of what we're making here, it's not so important whether it's true or not.

**ACTRESS.** What do you mean? To me it's crucial.

**DIRECTOR.** Since when?

**ACTRESS.** What do you mean since when? Since always.

**DIRECTOR.** What are you talking about, Julia?

**ACTRESS.** To me it's not the same if it happened to me or if it's something I wrote. Maybe it's something that happened to me, but precisely because it was an episode of amnesia, I don't remember it and then they tell me about it and I feel ashamed of myself afterwards, and the only way I can face the pain is through fiction, through the act of creating fiction.

*Something mysterious happens. Santos and María Luisa stare at her as if Fauna had suddenly materialized before them and José Luis is a bit frightened.*

DIRECTOR. I think it's best if we leave it for now and continue later. I'm exhausted . . . I buried two horses today.

SANTOS. One. I was the one who buried Lightning.


## V. TERROR

ACTRESS. Sometimes I feel like you use terror to try to keep us together.

DIRECTOR. What does that mean?

ACTRESS. Exactly that, it's like you treat me so badly that I can't leave you.

DIRECTOR. I don't understand.

ACTRESS. Of course you do. If you loved me and I were free, you'd be afraid that I would leave. So you instill fear in me so that I can't do anything other than stay, because I'm weak. I'm afraid. But that's not love.

DIRECTOR. I still don't understand what you're saying, but I know I don't like it.

ACTRESS. The image you create of me is almost always a negative reflection of who I am and I'm left trying to change it back so I can show you that in reality I'm better than what you see. And this is how you keep me with you. This lack of something, this constant feeling of being deficient makes me stay, but in a state of panic. And on top of that, while I spend my time trying to satisfy you, something that I'll never achieve, of course, because that's not what it's about, I'm unable to tell what or who it is that I myself desire. That's what I mean when I say that you keep me with you through terror. Because when you throw back an unbearable image of me, at the same time you instill the feeling in me that no other person could see me differently and that I should be grateful that you're still willing to put up with me.

**DIRECTOR.** You're crazy.

**ACTRESS.** You see? No, no, I'm not crazy.

**DIRECTOR.** You already told me that you don't want us to have a romantic relationship. You made that very clear. Also, what makes you think that I'd want to be with you here? Did you think that was a given? Really, what makes you think that I'm going to want to be with you at all? Why do you assume that? Do you think you're so irresistible?

**ACTRESS.** There it is—you're attacking me.

**DIRECTOR.** I'm attacking you. I'm attacking you? *I'm* attacking *you*? Please! You come here and drag me into who knows what ridiculousness, spouting a bunch of nonsense, saying that I terrify you, come on . . . that I bring out the worst in you; seriously Julia, are you even listening to the way you talk to me? You think you can say whatever you want to me.

**ACTRESS.** You're already out of control. Do you see what I mean?

**DIRECTOR.** I'm not out of control. It's just that you say the most ridiculous things. My God! I have a family; I'm not cut out for this shit. If we don't want to do this, let's not do it. Nobody's going to die.

**ACTRESS.** And this—what you're doing right now—you wouldn't call this terror.

**DIRECTOR.** Julia, don't bust my balls. Let me work in peace.

ACTRESS. How diplomatic.

DIRECTOR. What are you muttering about?

ACTRESS. Nothing. You're the kind of person who lashes out if you feel hurt.

DIRECTOR. Can we just keep working?

ACTRESS. Yes.

## VI. CONFUSED PEOPLE ARE DANGEROUS

*The four rehearse Fauna's confession scene in the Poets' Circle.*

SANTOS. Why do you want to be my mother?

ACTRESS. I don't want to be your mother. I want to tell your mother's story.

SANTOS. Which one?

ACTRESS. What do you mean which one? Her story—the story of her life.

SANTOS. Oh, her life, not one of her stories then.

ACTRESS. One of her stories . . . Ah no, no, right, no, her life.

SANTOS. Right. Why?

ACTRESS. Because it's fascinating. It fascinates me. And I think a lot of other people will think so, too. And I want to make this film so that other people will have the chance to know her.

SANTOS. Who?

ACTRESS. Your mother.

SANTOS. But my mother is dead.

ACTRESS. Yes, right, I know, that's why.

SANTOS. Right.

ACTRESS. Let's start again.

FIGURE 3.3 *Fauna*, Espacio Callejón, Buenos Aires, 2013. Actors (LEFT TO RIGHT): Esteban Bigliardi, Rafael Ferro, and Pilar Gamboa. *Photograph by Sebastián Arpesella.*

**SANTOS.** Yes.

**ACTRESS.** You start: "Pardon me, my good sir."

**SANTOS.** Yes. Pardon me, my good sir. It is not my intention to inconvenience you my dear friend, but I could not help but observe that there is a joining of forces in you that I am unable to discern.

**ACTRESS.** I don't know what you mean, my dear friend.

**SANTOS.** Do me the favor of not taking offense at my impertinence.

**ACTRESS.** Of course not, rest assured, proceed.

**SANTOS.** Well, my blessed friend, allow me to be truthful and forgive my clumsiness, but I proceed with the best of intentions. I do not wish to take advantage of or squander your time, but believe me when I say I do not know how to begin.

**ACTRESS.** My friend . . .

**SANTOS.** My beloved friend, I find that I am in love with you.

**ACTRESS.** Oh!

*Santos stops reading and kisses her. It seems as if he is improvising. Julia is disconcerted.*

**SANTOS.** Do I alarm you that much?

**ACTRESS.** What?

**SANTOS.** Why do you feel so threatened?

**ACTRESS.** Threatened? I don't know, no reason.

**SANTOS.** Really.

**ACTRESS.** Really what?

**SANTOS.** There's something that's bothering you.

(*Julia hugs him.*)

Calm down my dear friend, at my side you will have nothing to fear.

**MARÍA LUISA.** Be careful, Santos, the girl is getting confused and confused people are dangerous.

**SANTOS.** Really? Luisa, do you think that running away, avoiding everyone, being different, is an act of cowardice or courage?

**MARÍA LUISA.** Are you saying that because of her?

**SANTOS.** No, I'm saying it because of us, here.

**MARÍA LUISA.** Avoiding entanglements.

**SANTOS.** Yes.

**MARÍA LUISA.** I don't know. It depends on what your expectations or aspirations are. Fauna wouldn't be Fauno if she had shared her life with someone.

**SANTOS.** That's obvious. But does that make her brave or the opposite?

**ACTRESS.** How is it possible for a woman to do everything she has to do and be a woman at the same time?

**DIRECTOR.** I don't understand. Is that poetry?

**MARÍA LUISA.** Is that Fauna's?

**ACTRESS.** No! It's mine. What I'm asking is, what makes a woman a *woman*? Having or not having kids, being able to have them but choosing not to? Why can't a woman gestate a child outside of her body, give birth to a child without finding out about it? Why must a woman always inevitably know? How can I be an actress and be in my body and be a mother? How do I do it? How do I give my body to more than one thing? How can I split myself in two if I already do it all of the time? Divide myself into another being, another living being . . . I'm selfish either way—by being a mother or choosing never to be one. It's unavoidable. I want to be a father to my children. I want to conceive them far away from me, and not even know they exist, or know they exist but not have the need to see them all the time! What determines whether or not I'm a woman and what makes me act this way? Why this obsession with always knowing and understanding what is what and who makes whom? I can't relate anymore to this expectation of weakness.

**SANTOS.** I also feel weak.

**DIRECTOR.** So you want to make a film about women's issues?

**ACTRESS.** I want to be a father to my children.

**SANTOS.** Fauna was a father to us.

**ACTRESS.** Can we try the confession scene with Fauno read by a man? Would you be willing to try it?

**DIRECTOR.** If you think it will help.

**ACTRESS.** Yes. You start: "Pardon me, my good sir."

**SANTOS.** Yes. Pardon me, my good sir. It is not my intention to inconvenience you my dear friend, but I could not help but observe that there is a joining of forces in you that I am unable to discern.

**DIRECTOR.** I don't know what you mean, my dear friend.

**SANTOS.** Do me the favor of not taking offense at my impertinence.

**DIRECTOR.** Of course not, rest assured, proceed.

**SANTOS.** Well, my blessed friend, allow me to be truthful and forgive my clumsiness, but I proceed with the best of intentions. I do not wish to take advantage of or squander your time, but believe me when I say I do not know how to begin.

**DIRECTOR.** My friend . . .

**SANTOS.** My beloved friend, I find that I am in love with you.

**DIRECTOR.** Oh!

*José Luis kisses Santos. He hugs him.*

**MARÍA LUISA.** This script is terrible. Who wrote it?

**DIRECTOR.** I did.

**ACTRESS.** Your Fauno is more feminine than mine.


## VII. GENDER

**ACTRESS.** Luisa, would it be a problem for you, for the evolution of our work, if I confessed that I feel attracted to you?

**MARÍA LUISA.** Attracted?

**ACTRESS.** Yes, in a broad sense: aesthetic, moral . . . romantic.

**MARÍA LUISA.** Isn't it a little premature?

**ACTRESS.** I'm not sure. Not for me. Do you think it might be a problem?

**MARÍA LUISA.** Not for me.

**ACTRESS.** Oh, Luisa, what a relief. I was afraid I was in this alone.

**MARÍA LUISA.** Alone in what?

**ACTRESS.** In this, how I feel, what's happening to me, this . . . attraction, for lack of a better term.

**MARÍA LUISA.** Oh, well yes, you are alone in your attraction.

**ACTRESS.** Oh.

**MARÍA LUISA.** I don't want to hurt you, but I can't think of you sexually, as a sexual surface.

**ACTRESS.** Sexual surface?

**MARÍA LUISA.** On which to project myself, my desire, on which to project my desire.

**ACTRESS.** Oh, okay, I'm not sure what to say. I'm so sorry I thought we were on the same page. If not, I wouldn't have put myself out there.

**MARÍA LUISA.** I can't think of you as a woman.

**ACTRESS.** Oh.

**MARÍA LUISA.** This is all very stimulating. Don't take it the wrong way.

**ACTRESS.** No, no, forgive me for being so forward.

**MARÍA LUISA.** I'm confused about my mother.

**ACTRESS.** In what way?

**MARÍA LUISA.** With you playing the part of my mother.

**ACTRESS.** Oh, I see. Is it painful for you?

**MARÍA LUISA.** No, not in theory, I wouldn't say that, but it would be impossible for me to think of her sexually.

**ACTRESS.** Ah, yes, of course. I understand . . . What a shame.

**MARÍA LUISA.** Ah, what a flirt you are. But you are very beautiful.

**ACTRESS.** A lot of good that's done me.

**MARÍA LUISA.** Ah, no, well it's not that it does good—but it adorns.

**ACTRESS.** It fills in.

MARÍA LUISA. It embellishes.

ACTRESS. Hardly.

MARÍA LUISA. It confuses.

ACTRESS. In the best of cases.

## VIII. BETWEEN BOYS

SANTOS. Why doesn't she want you anymore?

DIRECTOR. Julia?

SANTOS. The actress.

DIRECTOR. Where did you hear that she doesn't want me? (*Their eyes meet, having just finished eavesdropping on the women.*) Besides, I stopped loving her first.

SANTOS. Oh, yeah?

DIRECTOR. Yeah.

SANTOS. Congratulations, then.

DIRECTOR. I don't get it.

SANTOS. I'm congratulating you on being the winner.

DIRECTOR. Ah, now I understand—irony.

SANTOS. Yes.

DIRECTOR. So, can I be honest with you?

SANTOS. Yeah.

DIRECTOR. I never stopped wanting her, I'm in love with her.

SANTOS. I know.

DIRECTOR. Oh, really? Is it that obvious?

(OVERLEAF) **FIGURE 3.4** *Fauna*, Espacio Callejón, Buenos Aires, 2013. Actor: Esteban Bigliardi. *Photograph by Sebastián Arpesella.*

SANTOS. Yes. . . .and I like you.

(*José Luis laughs, a lot.*)

I'm being serious.

DIRECTOR. Oh, really?

SANTOS. Yes.

DIRECTOR. But you seem so rough.

SANTOS. I am rough. And I'm attracted to you, in spite of your weakness.

DIRECTOR. I'm weak?

SANTOS. Yes.

DIRECTOR. I suppose I might be. Who are you? Where did you all come from?

SANTOS. Us? From nowhere, we've always been here. It was you two who came looking for us.

DIRECTOR. That's not what I mean. I don't mean it literally. Why is it so hard to make myself understood in this place?

SANTOS. Is it difficult?

DIRECTOR. Yes, very. Julia insisted on bringing me here, and I showed up not even knowing who Fauna was. I had never even heard her name. I like fiction. When it comes to this stuff, these biopics, I have no idea. I like writing a script, thinking about the screenplay as artificial, completely fictional and shooting it, even if it does end up resembling a real life when it's finished.

SANTOS. When what's finished?

DIRECTOR. The film.

SANTOS. Ah, right.

DIRECTOR. But I can't be a part of this, not like this, it's just not worth it.

SANTOS. Worth it?

DIRECTOR. Yeah, it seems like a high price to pay, and for what I'm not sure. Right now, I feel like I'm paying a very high price.

SANTOS. Are you saying that because of us?

DIRECTOR. Just look at me.

SANTOS. It looks to me like you're doing pretty well.

DIRECTOR. I have nothing.

SANTOS. What?

DIRECTOR. Just that—I have nothing, not even symbolic capital. I could have never gotten here if it wasn't for her. I'm a fraud.

SANTOS. Because of Fauna?

DIRECTOR. Because of Julia. Okay, yes, Fauna, too. I don't understand how things resonate. I don't have that ability, that disposition. Julia does—she feels things, she's awake, she perceives them, she understands. I don't know where she gets this unshakable intuition that drives her to pursue things. I really trust this sense she has and when I see her determination I follow her. Like right now, for example. That's how we got here.

SANTOS. I understand what you're saying but it doesn't seem so important to know who discovered what thing first. What's clear is that you're here, the same as her, doing research on your film, trying to get closer to the figure of Fauna.

DIRECTOR. But the whole Fauna thing isn't even true.

SANTOS. What's not true?

DIRECTOR. Fauno, Fauna, it's all a myth.

SANTOS. What exactly isn't true?

DIRECTOR. That she existed.

SANTOS. What do you mean? Where did that come from?

DIRECTOR. Julia invented all of it so she could be the center of attention.

**SANTOS.** Are you referring to the movie?

**DIRECTOR.** No, to your mother. Didn't you see her just now strutting around, dressed like her, bewitching us all? I already know her ways.

**SANTOS.** She's an actress.

**DIRECTOR.** Exactly.

**SANTOS.** She's acting.

**DIRECTOR.** Precisely. Don't believe any of it.

**SANTOS.** What do you mean?

**DIRECTOR.** All of this about Fauna.

**SANTOS.** But that was my mother.

**DIRECTOR.** No, no, no.

**SANTOS.** Yes, yes, yes, I assure you—yes. I don't understand when you got so confused.

**DIRECTOR.** I don't know, I'd say that I'm seeing things quite clearly.

**SANTOS.** Just a minute ago, I told you that I was in love with you and it fell on deaf ears.

**DIRECTOR.** Yeah, you're right, forgive me, but, the thing is, I can't deal with that information right now.

**SANTOS.** There is nothing to deal with.

**DIRECTOR.** Or to say, that's what I mean.

**SANTOS.** Then don't say anything. José Luis, before when we were burying the horses—didn't you realize the way I was looking at you?

**DIRECTOR.** You were looking at me?

**SANTOS.** Yes.

**DIRECTOR.** No, no, no, I was very focused.

**SANTOS.** And sad.

DIRECTOR. Yes, that too. But really I was more moved than sad. It was
such a shame, those enormous horses . . . I still can't quite grasp
how those insects could have overpowered such large animals.

SANTOS. It was a lot of bees. And the horses were tied up. That's what
killed them. It was our fault, an unforgivable mistake.

DIRECTOR. Well, these things happen.

SANTOS. No.

DIRECTOR. No?

SANTOS. No, they don't happen. I'm never going to forget this. I was
there when Lightning was born. Not only was I there but I helped
deliver her. One of her hooves was caught and she cried and the
mother neighed and tried to get away with the foal hanging
between her legs. Luisa had to keep her still while I opened the
way for Lightning . . . and that's how I helped her come into the
world. I practically birthed her and now I wasn't there when she
died, I couldn't help her die. And not only that but I killed her. I
killed her. It's as if nature insisted on completing what it proposed
at birth, what I had interrupted because the moment the mother,
the mare, started walking, she decided that her child would stay
tangled and like that the two would die together. It was in that
birth that both of them were fated to leave this earth together, and
I stopped it in a moment of reckless pride. I believed I could
reverse everything, but no, finally the two lie together, in the forest
and it's my fault I couldn't do anything to prevent it.

*The director embraces him and it's all very confusing.*

*Everyone is dressed like Julia, as poets.*

ACTRESS. There once was a man who had eleven sons and one daughter. One day, the children's mother dies and the man, feeling alone, marries another woman, who hates the twelve children profoundly. So the stepmother turns the boys into swans and forces them to leave, but her spell only works during the day. At nightfall they turn back into boys and they have to be on firm ground when this happens. If darkness ever catches them flying over water they fall to their deaths. Elisa, who is the only daughter, is banished to the forest by her father, who fails to recognize her after her stepmother paints her face with an evil ointment. The girl embarks on a pilgrimage to the coast to find her swan brothers. She walks day and night until she reaches the sea and there she waits. At sunset she sees a flock of eleven wild birds, and as the last ray of light disappears, there before her appear her eleven brothers. They tell her that the only way they will be freed from the curse is if she knits each of them a jacket made of nettles, a task she must complete in silence. Elisa spends the night with her brothers and promises them she'll begin knitting at dawn. She works tirelessly and quietly day and night. But one night, she's caught trying to steal nettles from a monastery. She's thrown in a dungeon, put on trial for witchcraft and found guilty because she refuses to break her vow of silence. She's on the verge of desperation because there's very little time left to finish the jackets. Suddenly she realizes nettle plants have begun to grow through the wet dungeon floor. She knits and knits away until the day of her sentence. Even as they drag her to the pyre she continues knitting. She's still working on the last of the eleven jackets when the flames reach her. At that moment, the eleven wild swans descend from the sky, and Elisa, already enveloped in smoke, throws the jackets to the swans. The instant they make contact with the nettles, one by one they turn into men. The townspeople witness the miracle in silence. The feathers fall from the young men, putting out the fire that threatened to engulf Elisa. Only the youngest brother, whose jacket was yet incomplete, reaches out to embrace his sister with an arm that is half human and half bird.[5]

*Santos approaches José Luis.*

SANTOS. Pardon me, my good sir. It is not my intention to inconvenience you my dear friend, but I could not help but observe that there is a joining of forces in you that I am unable to discern.

DIRECTOR. I don't know what you mean, my dear friend.

SANTOS. Do me the favor of not taking offense at my impertinence.

DIRECTOR. Of course not, rest assured, proceed.

SANTOS. Well, my blessed friend, allow me to be truthful and forgive my clumsiness, but I proceed with the best of intentions. I do not wish to take advantage of or squander your time, but believe me when I say I do not know how to begin.

DIRECTOR. My friend. . .

SANTOS. My beloved friend, I find that I am in love with you.

DIRECTOR. Oh!

*José Luis waits for a kiss but it doesn't come.*

SANTOS. I know this might seem rather unorthodox or unexpected, but please don't be scared.

DIRECTOR. No, not in the least. It doesn't scare me.

SANTOS. Oh, no?

5 Inspired by Hans Christian Andersen's fairy tale, *The Wild Swans.*

DIRECTOR. I've developed the same feelings for you, or to be more exact, this same feeling.

SANTOS. If I may, your arrival in this, in our circle, has started a revolution. You've energized us with your iconoclasm, your hunger and your candid spirit. So much so that the last thing I want to do is keep you at a distance, from me or from us, because of these feelings of mine, both personal and possessive. Take my words as a compliment and do with them what you find most prudent. Forgive me if I torment you, I've been treasuring these feelings and holding them close to my heart. You've become indispensable, my dear Fauno.

DIRECTOR (*looking at the women, as if desiring privacy*). Would you mind joining me on the patio for a few minutes?

SANTOS. No sir, it would be my pleasure to do so.

*They both step forward.*

DIRECTOR. My beloved Ramón, I haven't been totally honest with you.

SANTOS. I had a feeling.

DIRECTOR. No, but it's not what you think.

SANTOS. Oh, no?

DIRECTOR. No. I hope I won't hurt you and that you'll find a way to forgive me. It's a decision that I made before I met you.

SANTOS. Yes, yes, of course, neither of us was born yesterday, of course. I think I'm ready to hear what you have to say.

DIRECTOR. Santos, Ramón, I'm not Fauno. I'm Fauna.

SANTOS. What?

DIRECTOR. I'm not a man. I'm a woman.

*Julia appears and José Luis moves away.*

ACTRESS. I'm not a man. I'm a woman.

**SANTOS.** Ah, yes, yes, I see, of course, yes.

**ACTRESS.** Aren't you surprised?

**SANTOS.** Not really, to be honest, no.

**ACTRESS.** But what do you mean, "no"?

**SANTOS.** No. As a woman you couldn't have participated in our evening gatherings, that's why you dressed like this.

**ACTRESS.** Yes, but did you already know? Is this something that happens frequently?

**SANTOS.** No, and no, and yet it doesn't surprise me.

**ACTRESS.** Are you disappointed?

**SANTOS.** No, not at all.

**ACTRESS.** So, what then?

*Julia starts to get a bit worried, looks to one side, as if seeking support from either of them.*

**SANTOS.** I knew it this whole time.

**ACTRESS.** What is it exactly that you knew?

**SANTOS.** That you were an impostor, "Fauna."

**ACTRESS.** But didn't you say that it didn't surprise you? I don't understand.

**SANTOS.** It's not that it surprises me. It demoralizes me.

**ACTRESS.** What's happening right now?

**SANTOS.** What don't you understand? You don't love that man.

**ACTRESS.** My husband?

**SANTOS.** That one (*gesturing toward José Luis*).

**ACTRESS.** He's not my husband. That's Fauno.

**SANTOS.** That's José Luis.

**ACTRESS.** Uh, did we cut already?

SANTOS. No, you listen to me, fake little Fauna.

ACTRESS. I don't understand why you're talking to me like this.

SANTOS. I said listen don't speak. Listen . . . There's only one Fauna here. We don't need another one. There will never be another one like her and it's a perverted gesture to try and emulate her for something as frivolous as a film.

ACTRESS. Frivolous?

SANTOS. You want to portray my mother, represent her, be her?

ACTRESS. I want to tell her story.

SANTOS. What story?

ACTRESS. The story of her life.

SANTOS. There's no such thing as telling the story of a life. That's for people who don't know how to live. Instead of telling her story, why don't you tell your story, the story of your own life, something that you know about.

ACTRESS. I don't think my life is that interesting.

SANTOS. Exactly, it's not.

ACTRESS. My life?

SANTOS. The life of an actor. I don't know you well enough to judge you.

ACTRESS. Okay, so, what happens now?

SANTOS. What I want is for you to leave this place without a trace.

ACTRESS. And go where?

SANTOS. I'm not sure where, wherever you want, just vanish, no need to explain.

ACTRESS. Okay, I don't understand. Even if this is a joke, it's not funny. I don't like it. I don't like it at all.

SANTOS. I'm being very serious, more serious than I've been all night long.

**ACTRESS.** But I was acting.

**SANTOS.** Yes, the entire time.

**ACTRESS.** No, not the entire time, just now and earlier, but not anymore.

**SANTOS.** I don't believe you, now you're acting like a fragile actress.

**ACTRESS.** I'm not fragile!

**SANTOS.** How can you prove that? How do we know?

**ACTRESS.** I'm not sure where you're going with this.

**SANTOS.** I'm not going anywhere. You're the one who's going.

**ACTRESS.** And if I refuse?

**DIRECTOR.** Come on, Julia. Let's go.

**MARÍA LUISA.** Now I get it. This is like in *Saverio the Cruel*. Do you know *Saverio the Cruel*? By Roberto Arlt? It's like Calderón but with a sad ending. Will this have a sad ending too?

**SANTOS.** Sad for whom?

**MARÍA LUISA.** That's a good question, sad for whom . . . "When my head was filled with clouds, I believed that a funny little ghost could protect me against a crude reality. But now I realize that one hundred ghosts are not worth one man's life. Before meeting you all I was a happy man . . . At night I would return to my quarters extremely tired. To make a living I had to reinvent myself so many times that I inevitably ended up overestimating my personality. When you invited me to participate in the farce, because I was unaccustomed to such splendid dreams, the farce transformed my sensibility into a violent reality that steadily modified the architecture of my life."[6]

---

6 Roberto Arlt, *Teatro completo* (Buenos Aires: Schapire, 1968), p. 75.

**SANTOS**. I like the part about the architecture of one's life. Is that *Saverio?*

**MARÍA LUISA**. Yes, the deceived—deceiver—deceived.

**SANTOS**. "Reality is cruel if stripped of all sense of transcendence, if one lives a life that is impossible to change . . . The cruelest thing about reality is not it's potential to be cruel, but the fact that reality itself is inevitable."[7]

**MARÍA LUISA**. Absolutely.

*The four Faunas say I love you. María Luisa says it to Santos and hesitates when saying it to Julia. Santos says it to José Luis and hesitates with Julia. José Luis says it to Julia and hesitates with Santos. Julia says it to María Luisa and hesitates with José Luis.*

THE END

---

**7** Enrique Carpintero, *La alegría de lo necesario. Las pasiones y el poder en Spinoza y Freud* (Buenos Aires: Topia, 2007), p. 135.

REWILDING

*Rewilding* was commissioned by and premiered at TACEC (Teatro Argentino Centro de Experimentación y Creación), La Plata, Argentina in 2016. The play was directed by Romina Paula with assistant direction by Gladys Escudero, set and lighting design by Matías Sendón, painting by Denise Groesman, production management by Maxi Libera, and with artistic collaboration by Sebastían Arpesella.

## CAST

| | |
|---:|---|
| GABI | Denise Groesman |
| MARÍA | Agostina Luz López |
| JOSÉ ANTONIO | Esteban Bigliardi |

# Rewilding

TRANSLATED BY **April Sweeney** AND **Brenda Werth**

". . . what I wanted to find in the painting,
I found only between myself and the painting"
—Heinrich von Kleist
on Caspar David Friedrich's *Seelandschaft*[1]

## I. JOSÉ ANTONIO

*Gabi dances. The creole waltz "José Antonio," written by Chabuca Granda (1968) with vocals by Lucha Reyes (1970) plays in the background. María watches her.*

## II. KASPER HAUSER

*José Antonio is lying on the floor, motionless but with his eyes open. Gabi and María are standing next to him, observing him. María examines him, she takes the watch he's holding in his hand and puts it on. She gives him a hug. Meanwhile, Gabi keeps a lookout. Gabi does a basic vision test and has him follow her finger with his eyes. Finally, José Antonio gets up.*

## III. IT'S NOT THE ORIGINAL

*Gabi tells María a story. José Antonio looks at the painting.*

**GABI.** My brother, the one from the mountains, is not my real brother. There's *something* in his body, something that replaced him. Many

---

1 Heinrich Von Kleist, *Sämtliche Werke und Briefe in 6 Bänden* (Wilhelm Herzog ed.) (Leipzig: Im Insel Verlag, 1910), p. 167.

years ago, he disappeared into the woods and never returned. What I mean is, he came back but it wasn't him. It's not that he was different, or that he'd changed. He was something else entirely. An other that invaded our family and devoured it from the inside out.

It was April 13th. I remember the date clearly because it's my mother's birthday. It fell on a Sunday that year and we were at a barbecue at the rest stop right off of Route 9, heading north. On Sundays the rest stops usually fill up with people who park their cars under the trees and spend the whole day there listening to the game on their car radios with the doors open. But that Sunday there was almost nobody there. Just one couple that ate and left early.

Anyway, behind the grills, if you crossed the barbed wire, was the woods. It was a grove of evergreens that had been fed by the runoff from the canal and the ground was blanketed with dead pine needles. About a hundred meters into the grove the place became ugly, with shards of glass sticking out of the mud, rusted sheet metal, the decomposing corpses of bloated dogs, and rats the size of cats prowling around in the refuse. What occupied the body of my brother came from there.

There's a photo from that afternoon. I keep it because it marks the exact moment in which everything began to deteriorate. There we are, the four of us, in front of the trees. To one side you can see the back of the light blue Dodge. My mother is still young and has one eye closed as the sun strikes her face. A smoldering cigarette hangs from my father's fingers. My brother smiles, the headphones of his Walkman draped loosely around his neck. It's a marvelous smile, a smile that says: look at me, I'm seventeen years old; I'm new to the world; I'm full of fire. His smile is frozen in that picture. It's the last time we'll see it.

**FIGURE 4.1** *Rewilding/Cimarrón*, Teatro Nacional Argentino–Teatro Cervantes, Buenos Aires, July 2017. Actors (LEFT TO RIGHT): Esteban Bigliardi, Denise Groesman, and Agostina Luz López. *Photograph by Sebastián Arpesella.*

After the photo, we ate the cake and my parents fell asleep on some lawn chairs. I sat against a tree and started to read a comic book. I didn't notice what my brother was doing. Ten or fifteen minutes went by. That's when my mother opened her eyes and asked where he was, her brow furrowed with worry. Maybe she'd had a nightmare or one of her premonitions. She looked at me and I shrugged. She went over to the barbed wire and called for him. My mother yelled his name several times. She woke my father and the three of us called for him. Then we heard the snap of a branch breaking and my brother emerged from the grove with his Walkman on. He just stood there staring at us. When I think of that expression I feel cold.[2]

## IV. I AM VERY HAPPY

*José Antonio repeats the same sentence several times, with difficulty, in different ways and in different positions. It's as if he were learning how to speak. He says it to María, Gabi, and the painting.*

**JOSÉ ANTONIO.** I am very happy that you are here.

## V. LATE, BY SARAH RUHL

**MARÍA.** In the play, she's a girl cowboy. Although that sounds like a contradiction because she's not a boy but a girl. You see, initially cowboy work was done only by men, the word itself originally concerns the work of boys. Anyway, the girl cowboy didn't take care of horses. She broke them. She was a horse trainer and she talked about horses all the time. That's something I don't really understand because as far as I know a cowboy herds cows, as the name implies. Or is it *now* that a cowboy is anyone who wears a hat and rides a horse?

**JOSÉ ANTONIO.** It's a character that's associated more with the wild West. I'm more familiar with it from fiction, to be honest with you. But I think that my definition of all things American comes from fiction.

**GABI.** American or North American?

---

2 Excerpt from short story by Luciano Lamberti: "La canción que cantábamos todos los días," in *El loro que podía adivinar el futuro* (Buenos Aires: Editorial Nudista, 2019).

**JOSÉ ANTONIO.** American, North American.

**MARÍA.** It's all the same.

**GABI.** No.

**JOSÉ ANTONIO.** At one point they were the same. They weren't the same, but it didn't matter.

**MARÍA.** Well, no, no, it's not that it doesn't matter. Anyway, let me go on. In the play she's masculine and a little marginalized. Actually, she is literally marginalized because she lives on the outskirts of the city in a stable with her horses. But it's not like it is here, where you have to travel hundreds of miles before it becomes country. The way it is there, at least from how they talk in the play, it's understood that the plains, where the girl-boy lived, were almost like the suburbs of the town where the main character lived with her husband. And while I was reading, I imagined a small city, a rural town like the one from *Brokeback Mountain*: a couple of houses, businesses, the main street and then a rural expanse.

**GABI.** Like a movie.

**MARÍA.** Like a movie, yeah. And it's also North American, like the movie. But in the play, the main character and this woman, called Red, like the color, meet again and they begin to develop a bond, a nice friendship. At the same time, the main character and her childhood sweetheart start their lives together. They get married and have a child, who is XXY. The play follows several years of the lives of these people. Over the course of the play, the relationship between the main character and her husband begins to deteriorate and the other relationship, the one between her and Red, remains strong. Or honestly, I'm not sure. And I think what happens is that they have their child, who is XXY, operated on to try and define her as a girl but of course it's only a temporary fix until the hormones kick in. The father is determined to raise her as a daughter and reinforce her identity as a girl but the mother isn't. The mother wants her to know that originally she was both and neither, something in between, and that she shouldn't feel strange about it and that she'll be able to choose. Or maybe she'll choose not to choose. That's another reason for the rift in their relationship. The end of the play isn't entirely clear to me. I think it insinuates that the main character raises her child with Red on the outskirts of town but it's not so clear. The play ends with all three of them looking at the horses, or something like that, but I don't know if that necessarily means that she abandoned her husband.

GABI. I would have liked nothing more than to belong, to be able to choose these things. But in the schoolyard I didn't feel like I belonged either on the team wearing pants or the team wearing skirts. I think people read me as being rebellious, but it was nothing more than perplexity.


## VI. DER SCHIMMELREITER / THE RIDER ON THE WHITE HORSE[3]

GABI. Is German your first language?

MARÍA. He is German.

GABI. Okay, but you grew up here, right?

JOSÉ ANTONIO. Yeah, I grew up here. I'm bilingual. German is my mother tongue.

MARÍA. Mother tongue is something you say in all languages, right? The nation is paternal, and the language is maternal?

GABI. It's the *madre patria*.

JOSÉ ANTONIO. So, white horses aren't called anything special, you just say *white horse*, right?

---

**3** Theodor Storm's 1888 novella *Der Schimmelreiter* [The rider on the white horse] is also commonly translated as *The Dykemaster*.

GABI. As far as I know, yes.

MARÍA. What do you say in German?

JOSÉ ANTONIO. *Schimmel. Schimmel* is also what you call the mold that grows on bread or food. Do you know what I'm talking about?

MARÍA. The green fuzz?

JOSÉ ANTONIO. Exactly. Exactly. This kind of horse has a white coat with gray spots like halos.

MARÍA. Oh, yeah.

GABI. According to legend, these horses are cursed and ridden by the devil.

MARÍA. Really?

JOSÉ ANTONIO. Yeah, that I knew. It's one of the reasons they crucified me.

GABI. Literally?

JOSÉ ANTONIO. No, not literally . . .

GABI. Right.

JOSÉ ANTONIO. There was a conventional understanding of levees and how they were made, an older construction that had been used for decades, but it had its disadvantages. The levee I designed was more . . . how should I put it . . . gradual? Less abrupt? With a less pronounced slope. I understand that at first glance it might leave you feeling vulnerable because it's unassuming; it doesn't look like a big block or a wall. But you can't combat the sea with a wall, it just won't work.

MARÍA. Why not?

JOSÉ ANTONIO. It needs to be contained by something with a more dynamic form, something that mimics the movement of the sea. If not, the weight always falls on the same section and sooner or later the wall breaks.

**GABI.** But not with a more dynamic design?

**JOSÉ ANTONIO.** It can still happen, but with a more dynamic design the levee will last hundreds of years longer.

**GABI.** And they didn't approve it?

**JOSÉ ANTONIO.** They didn't have a choice. But it had a tragic end. Do you know the story?

(*Both shake their heads.*)

We built a new levee based on my design. Not without incident of course. At one point, I discovered some workers trying to bury a live dog, a tradition, apparently, to ensure the stability of the levee. But we built my levee without offering anything and it still held up. And what's more, we had years of prosperity, because thanks to the levee, a large plot of land that used to be a mud hole turned into a fertile, gleaming meadow. It was ploughed and sown. It was good, young soil, until one summer there was a storm that lasted for days and the water rose.

**GABI.** The levee didn't hold.

**JOSÉ ANTONIO.** Oh no, it definitely held. My levee was infallible, I assure you. What didn't hold was the remaining section of the old levee that they had refused to replace. All of the weight of that swell of water crashed down on that wall, and it held as long as possible until it couldn't anymore.

**MARÍA.** And then?

**JOSÉ ANTONIO.** It broke and everything flooded and washed away.

**GABI.** Except for your levee.

**JOSÉ ANTONIO.** Except for my levee. It resisted, which ended up being worse, because now it's the only thing left standing, ruins protruding from the mud like a deformed face that nobody wants to see again, including me.

*The three dance the waltz "Qué importa," by Lucha Reyes.[4] Just the first minute of the song, the introduction and the first stanza: "One more failure / What does it matter? / If in life I was never happy anyway. / Yet one more heartbreak / Is just another drop in the ocean for me, / One more failure, / What does it matter?"*

## VIII. SOLIDARITY

**JOSÉ ANTONIO.** Why do winners always act as if they deserve to win? Using the verb "to win" is the foundational error. Does one win elections? Or is one simply elected? Is it a competition? Do you win? What do you win? The right to govern. You win a huge number of responsibilities and obligations. If we were dealing with serious people, they would be very worried about the prospect of "winning." And then what? We become responsible for all of these people? Oh god. Nobody in their right mind would want that. Nobody. When I was young, at summer camp, we held a mock election, like a game. We split up into parties, we wrote speeches, we campaigned for a couple of days. When election time came, it was clear that our party was not favored to win but we had to persevere. We voted in a tent. They tallied the votes. There were six of us and we only received five votes. We were one short. We were confused, concerned, until one of the guys confessed that he had voted for a different party. He said that he realized that winning would be too much work and that he preferred to defer to others. We perceived this as an act of betrayal of the highest order.

**MARÍA.** When I was a teenager, I took a road trip with my father and he hit someone with his car. We were going fast and a body flashed

---

**4** Lucha Reyes, "Qué importa" [What does it matter?, 1970]. Lyrics by Juan Mosto.

in front of us. My father couldn't stop and crashed right into it. At first we didn't understand what had happened. We got out of the car and saw him lying on the pavement, rigid, with his eyes open. He said, "My name is José," and he moved slightly. My father helped him get up. He was able to stand without much effort, which was sort of strange given the blow he'd received. It took some convincing but my father finally persuaded him to let us take him to the next exit.

GABI. So he rode with you?

MARÍA. We drove with him for a long stretch, yes. And I was lucky enough to fall in love briefly, for the duration of the trip, and a couple of days after that.

GABI. Was he young?

MARÍA. Like my father. He was an anarchist.

JOSÉ ANTONIO. Your father?

MARÍA. No, José. The other José. The man.

GABI. What do you mean that he was an anarchist?

MARÍA. He called himself an anarchist. He sparred with my father, who was a Peronist. My father thought he was lazy, the kind of person who presents himself as a freelance worker but who really just prefers not to work.

JOSÉ ANTONIO. An anarchist, right.

MARÍA. It definitely affected my reunion with my father. It happened at the beginning of our vacation; we hadn't seen each other for years, aside from a couple of hours here and there, and that's how it started, with us estranged, because of José.

GABI. Why did you become estranged?

MARÍA. Because I was fascinated by the things he said, by his philosophy of life, and I was appalled by my father's arrogant and conceited tone when speaking to him. What made it worse was that José responded so earnestly, laughing at his jokes, and that made me even more furious. It made me want to cry.

GABI. And what happened to José?

MARÍA. He disappeared. We stopped at a rest stop and he vanished into thin air. It was in an area that was totally desolate, in the middle of nowhere, and that's where he disappeared. Not even a glimpse of him walking off into the sunset. It was so strange. Maybe I got distracted for a moment, or maybe I fell asleep and then realized he wasn't there. My father didn't see him leave either. It's a mystery.

*Pause.*

JOSÉ ANTONIO. Could he have died?

GABI. That's what I wondered.

MARÍA. Why would you say that?

GABI. My dog was hit by a car near our house and walked home as if nothing had happened. After a couple of hours he collapsed and died from internal injuries.

MARÍA. Is that true?

GABI. Well, we think so, maybe . . . It was a dog.

JOSÉ ANTONIO. And your father?

MARÍA. No, my father's alive.

JOSÉ ANTONIO. Were you able to make amends?

MARÍA. Yes, fortunately, but it took some time. It turns out it was all just a big misunderstanding. I spent my whole childhood and a part of my teenage years mourning an absent father and in the end it was my mother who had kept him from seeing me, and he obeyed. Maybe that was his error. Apparently he used to hang around the school entrance, hoping to see me leave and have a few moments with me, so he wouldn't miss me as much. After a while he was allowed to take me out to eat every couple of months, but those outings were agony; I barely spoke to him because I thought he had left us. It was all a huge misunderstanding, and just thinking about it is painful. Luckily, we were able to reconstruct what happened and now we try to spend as much time as possible together. We have a good relationship, a much better one than the one I have with my mother. She was the one who taught me to see the world; she created an image of the world for me that I ended up not really liking. Do you know how much time it took for me to realize that? I'm still working through it.

GABI. She gave you the gift of gab.

MARÍA. Huh?

GABI. You're good at talking.

MARÍA. Maybe, but I think I owe that to my father, too.

JOSÉ ANTONIO. The father tongue, the motherland.

GABI. Sometimes I'm embarrassed when people state things that seem obvious to me, because I feel like if there's a need to prove something, then maybe it's not that obvious after all. The idea of stigmatizing someone, especially someone in a situation of vulnerability, really bothers me. If we focus on that vulnerability, if we talk about it, name it, doesn't it identify the person as weak? I feel like vindication always takes place from a position of power, and isn't that in itself a contradiction?

MARÍA. The powerful should always watch over the weak.

GABI. If things were fair, the powerful would empower the weak and give them power, not reinforce their weakness.

JOSÉ ANTONIO. You have to do what's right and that's that.

GABI. Yes, but according to what criteria?

**JOSÉ ANTONIO.** The criteria of love and art. The love of art. And poetry.

**GABI.** I agree but it's not really possible to talk like that anymore.

**JOSÉ ANTONIO.** No?

**MARÍA.** Nobody talks that way anymore.

**GABI.** You can't really talk about love, art, and poetry so simply without sounding foolish.

**JOSÉ ANTONIO.** Foolish?

**GABI.** Anything you say without cynicism runs the risk of being taken for naiveté.

*Gabi and María repeat the words love, art, and poetry several times.*

**JOSÉ ANTONIO.** Maybe you're thinking about it in the wrong away. There needs to be empathy. And it needs to correspond.

**GABI.** Correspond?

**JOSÉ ANTONIO.** Correspond.

**MARÍA.** Correspond to what?

**JOSÉ ANTONIO.** Correspond to the other, somehow.

"I received your letter just a few days ago. I thank you for your great confidence, so dear to me. This is about all I can do. I cannot apprehend the style of your verses; I reject any attempt at criticism. Nothing is further from touching a work of art than the words of a critic. Things are not as easy to grasp and pronounce as we would like to believe. Most acts are ineffable and are produced in a space not accessible to language. The most ineffable of all are works of art, whose mysterious existence endures, unlike ours, which ends.

"Works of art come from infinite solitude, and nothing reaches them less than criticism. Only love can grasp them, capture them and do them justice. Affirm your feelings in every argumentation, discussion, or introduction; if in error, the natural growth of your inner life will lead you to that recognition. Let your own judgments grow quietly, their development undisturbed, which, like all progress that comes from deep within, should not be forced or accelerated. Everything is maturing and then giving birth. Let each impression and each budding feeling develop in darkness, in what is unspeakable, unconscious, beyond the reach of our comprehension, and wait for a new clarity with profound patience and humility. This is what it means to live artistically, in understanding as in creating.

"There it is impossible to measure time, one year is nothing, and ten years are nothing. Being an artist means not adding or counting, maturing like a tree, not rushing the production of sap, and standing tall and calmly in spring storms, without fearing that summer might not come. Summer always arrives, but only for the patient ones, who remain there, as if eternity stretched out in front of them, unconcerned, silent, and vast. I learn it every day, I learn it with pain, for which I am grateful: patience is everything!"[5]

## IX. THE MACHINE OF GOD

**MARÍA.** What I'm afraid of is that everything could end without having done enough or the right thing.

**GABI.** What would that be like? What do you mean by everything ending?

**MARÍA.** The whole world, all of existence.

**GABI.** You mean death?

---

5 Romina Paula translates excerpts from Rainer Maria Rilke's *Letters to a Young Poet* (1929). Our English translation takes into account both the original German and Paula's Spanish translation. Rilke, *Briefe an einen jungen Dichter* (Göttingen: LIWI, 2019), p. 12.

MARÍA. Yes, but not really. It's not death that worries me, it's the idea that everything could end.

GABI. The world?

MARÍA. The world as we know it. Or rather, life on earth.

GABI. Ah.

MARÍA. A while back I read that in Switzerland they have a machine that accelerates time and generates black holes through which things can enter or disappear.

GABI. How does that work?

MARÍA. It allows things to travel from other dimensions into our own. Apparently in a city somewhere in Switzerland, they built a gigantic machine the size of several cathedrals with subterranean tunnels a hundred kilometers long, in an effort to reproduce some of the physical phenomena caused by the Big Bang. They wanted to confirm or reject the scientific paradigm we live in. I think that's what it was for. But some scientists warned that if they played god there was always a possibility that the universe might destabilize and explode. Or, for example, that the Earth might disappear entirely.

GABI. I don't understand what the machine does exactly.

MARÍA. I don't either, exactly. What I understood is that it accelerates things; it makes atoms or atom particles collide in order to prove things. And the resulting fission could destroy the world or open up black holes that could function as portals to other dimensions.

GABI. But are these hypotheses or real possibilities?

MARÍA. Both, I think.

GABI. Would the things that travel through the black holes necessarily be bad?

MARÍA. I don't know.

158

ROMINA PAULA

GABI. What could they be?

MARÍA. Beings? I don't know. I'm not sure if it's something as concrete as that or if it's something on a chemical level. That's something I still don't understand. They talked about visitors and the destruction of space and time, the collapse.

GABI. Collapse.

MARÍA. Collapse.

GABI. The weird thing is that I'm listening to you but what you're saying isn't scaring me. Actually, it almost gives me a feeling of possibility, of liberation.

MARÍA. Now that you say it, I feel that way too, deep down. But the thing is that in the article I read it was all super-apocalyptic. It's impressive, your ability to see the potential in something that could ruin your existence.

GABI. Is that what I'm doing?

MARÍA. Yes.

GABI. Nice.

MARÍA. The article also said that they had built the machine in that precise spot because there had been an open portal there since Roman times.

GABI. In Switzerland?

MARÍA. Yes, that's what it said, that there had been a temple dedicated to Apollo with a portal that led to the netherworld.

GABI. Are you still talking about the same machine?

MARÍA. Yes, but the thing with the machine is very real. It exists now, as we're talking about it here, and there are hundreds of scientists from all over the world who work there every day, who ride their bikes to work and eat sandwiches on their lunch breaks. Whereas the whole portal thing is a theory, whether it's a conspiracy or not, it's just a theory.

*They gaze at her, spellbound.*

GABI. You're charming.

MARÍA. What?

GABI. You—you exude charm.

MARÍA. I don't understand.

*The refrain of "La flor de la canela" by Lucha Reyes begins to play and Gabi sings to María.*[6]

GABI. That's Chabuca Granda again.

MARÍA. The one who's singing?

GABI. No, that's Lucha Reyes. Chabuca is the songwriter of this one. And of "José Antonio," the one we were dancing to earlier. Chabuca the rich one and Lucha the poor one, both from Lima.

MARÍA. They're both beautiful, the songs. Lucha and Chabuca, what names! And the line about exuding charm, what does that mean?

GABI. Just that, exuding charm, grace.

MARÍA. Charm. And how do you know them? The musicians?

GABI. My mother was a music lover and a great guitarist who was afraid of the guitar and her own voice.

MARÍA. What do you mean she was afraid?

GABI. She was a beautiful guitarist, not in a technical sense, but she was passionate and she was a singer, too. I spent my childhood listening to Latin American women singers. And I listened to her all the time when she was alive, no matter what I was doing.

MARÍA. And do you play anything?

---

6 Chabuca Granda, "La flor de la canela" [The cinnamon flower, 1950]. Vocals by Lucha Reyes (1970).

**GABI.** The guitar, but very poorly. More than anything I like to listen.

**MARÍA.** And did they know each other?

**GABI.** Who?

**MARÍA.** The Peruvians.

**GABI.** Lucha and Chabuca?

**MARÍA.** Ches . . . yes.

**GABI.** I'm not sure how well they knew each other, but they did know each other, yes. There is a photo of them. It's the only one I ever saw. In the photo they're seated next to each other on baroque high-backed chairs, holding hands.

(*They imitate the photo. Gabi is Chabuca and María is Lucha.*)

Lucha is brown-skinned and is dressed in white, and Chabuca is light-skinned and is dressed in black. They're both smiling. In reality it's Chabuca who's holding Lucha's hand on her lap. She holds her left hand over her lap, and they both look at the camera. Lucha's face is sincere. She looks and smiles, and that's it. Chabuca's chin is lifted slightly, giving her a slightly arrogant air, a distance, as if she were thinking about something else.

**MARÍA.** I like listening to you talk. I talk a lot.

**GABI.** Yeah, but it's nice.

**MARÍA.** Really?

**GABI.** Yeah. This isn't the first time we've met, is it?

**MARÍA.** I don't know. I don't think so.

**JOSÉ ANTONIO.** "You are so young, with everything ahead of you, and I wanted to ask you as best I can, that you be patient with everything that is unresolved in your heart, and that you try to love questions as if they were locked rooms or books written in another language. Do not try to find answers that can't be given to you yet because you haven't lived them. It's about living everything. Live the questions now. Perhaps gradually, without even realizing it, one day you may find you are inhabiting the answers.

"Sex is arduous, yes, because all things that have been assigned to us are arduous; almost everything serious is arduous, and everything is serious. If you recognize this and achieve a personal relationship with your sex (removed from custom and convention), then you will not fear losing yourself or feel unworthy of your best possession."[7]

**GABI.** And you? Where do you situate yourself? Beyond everything?

**JOSÉ ANTONIO.** Thither.

**GABI.** I'm sorry?

**MARÍA.** Another way of saying "there," but nobody uses it anymore.

**GABI.** Because I don't see you as being old enough or crotchety enough to situate yourself in the hereafter.

**JOSÉ ANTONIO.** I was quoting from Rilke's *Letters to a Young Poet*.

**MARÍA.** Just now?

**JOSÉ ANTONIO.** Yes, and also earlier. I'm not trying to situate myself in the hereafter. But I will admit that there is something about the funnel that is a profound relief to me.

**GABI.** What funnel?

**JOSÉ ANTONIO.** The one that measures the passage of time. The relief I feel when I'm made aware of the progressive reduction of my possibilities, of everything that I'm no longer able to do or be. I remember the abundance of possibilities of youth and it gives me vertigo.

**GABI.** And the funnel?

**MARÍA.** It's an image, right? That of reduction.

---

**7** Rilke, *Briefe an einen jungen Dichter*, pp. 14–15.

FIGURE 4.2 *Rewilding/Cimarrón*, Teatro Nacional Argentino–Teatro Cervantes, Buenos Aires, July 2017. Actors (LEFT TO RIGHT): Agostina Luz López, Esteban Bigliardi, and Denise Groesman. *Photograph by Sebastián Arpesella.*

JOSÉ ANTONIO. Yes, that's right. And in the present, to know that not even this, as small and precise as it may be, is possible to comprehend entirely. But this idea calms me, the ability to dedicate myself to the same thing without ever exhausting it, a constant practice. And the more my practice deepens the less I can see.

GABI. You're an architect?

MARÍA. And a painter.

**JOSÉ ANTONIO.** Hobbyist.

**GABI.** What do you paint?

**JOSÉ ANTONIO.** Landscapes.

**GABI.** Realism?

**JOSÉ ANTONIO.** I try to reproduce what I see.

**GABI.** In a realist vein?

**JOSÉ ANTONIO.** The effect is fairly real, yes.

**MARÍA.** They're a little gloomy. No offense.

**JOSÉ ANTONIO.** It doesn't offend me. It's just my way of seeing.

**MARÍA.** But they're beautiful. *And* they're beautiful, I should say. There's nothing wrong with gloominess in itself, I don't think.

**JOSÉ ANTONIO.** You're referring to negative beauty.

**GABI.** Is that a thing?

**JOSÉ ANTONIO.** Negative beauty? Of course. It's something like the sublime.

**MARÍA.** Sublime. Sublime in the grand sense?

**JOSÉ ANTONIO.** And sadness, too.

**MARÍA.** But doesn't the sublime have a positive connotation?

**JOSÉ ANTONIO.** It depends on what you consider positive. It's usually presented as the opposite of beauty in the sense that it's demanding of the person who experiences it. It's not a passive, contemplative feeling, like the one that beauty generates.

**MARÍA.** The sublime is sad then?

**GABI.** And dangerous.

**JOSÉ ANTONIO.** Exactly. It's dangerous, threatening. It attacks your life. That's why I am sticking with the sublime in art, because it offers all of the advantages of nature and none of its inconveniences.

**MARÍA.** One day, near my house, a man appeared out of nowhere. Nobody knew where he came from, not even he himself. One day he just showed up at the main plaza, sitting on a bench in silence with his eyes wide open. He was well dressed and had an overall nondescript appearance with his hair groomed and his nails trimmed. A crowd began to form around him, and the first person who approached him was a boy, who reached out to touch him. The man didn't even react. The boy asked him what his name was and the only word the man knew how to say was "steed." And because the boy didn't know what steed meant, he ran around yelling that the person who had just arrived was called Steed. And the name stuck and everyone called him that from then on. The first thing they did was bring him to the local authorities, but he didn't utter a word. They wanted him to draw a picture but the only thing he drew were lines and squiggles, nothing figurative, nothing with a narrative. So they put him in a home and one of the nurses who cared for him took pity on him and began to teach him to speak. He didn't know how. It was as if he were a newborn, a *tabula rasa*. She taught him everything she knew and Steed eventually began to write simple sentences. Every once and a while someone appeared looking for a lost loved one who had gone missing and had similar features. A few times someone was close to identifying him, but in the end he was never the missing person they were looking for. So Steed stayed there, growing old in his new house. At some point the woman took him home to live with her and they became something like a couple, or a mother and son, I don't know exactly what kind of relationship they had, and it also doesn't matter. They looked happy together. Every afternoon she took Steed out for a walk and they stopped at the bench where he first appeared, and they stayed there for a moment, sitting quietly. Sometimes she had tea, other times no. He never had anything, he just remained quiet and unfazed.[8]

*María approaches José Antonio and returns his watch to him.*

## XI. LETTERS TO A YOUNG RILKE

*José Antonio is standing, just like in the beginning. Gabi reads from a book and María listens. It's almost as if it were an epitaph for José Antonio.*

**GABI.** "One day, someday there will exist a young girl and a woman whose name will no longer mean the opposite of masculinity, but something on its own, something that is envisioned without a complement, without a boundary, but just as existence and life: the feminine human being.

"And in man there is also maternity, it seems, physical and spiritual: his way of conceiving is also a form of giving birth, and he gives birth when he creates from deep within. And it is likely that genders are more related than what people say, and that the great renewal of the world perhaps resides in that men and women, liberated from all confusion and reluctance, will not seek each other as opposites but as siblings and neighbors and they will come together as human beings, to bear together and with seriousness and patience the burden of the sex that has been imposed on them.

"This progress will transform the experience of love, which has gone astray. It will be a foundational change and will give it the form of a thoughtful relationship, no longer one between a man and a woman but rather between human beings."[9]

THE END

---

8 Inspired by the story of Kaspar Hauser, a young man who claimed to have grown up in isolation in the forest near Nuremberg, Germany, and whose life has been the subject of many artistic works, including Werner Herzog's 1974 film *The Enigma of Kaspar Hauser*.

9 Rilke, *Briefe an einen jungen Dichter*, p. 16.

moment, sitting quietly. Sometimes she had tea, other times no. He never had anything, he just remained quiet and unfazed.[8]